EA[R]
CHRISTIANITY
33 C.E. - 330 C.E.

APOSTOLIC, APOLOGIST
AND CHURCH FATHERS

CHRISTIAN
PUBLISHING HOUSE

EARLY CHRISTIANITY 33 C.E.—330 C.E.

Apostolic, Apologist and Church Fathers

Edward D. Andrews

ISBN-13: 978-0615844923

ISBN-10: 0615844928

Christian Publishing Houses

Cambridge, Ohio

EARLY CHRISTIANITY 33 C.E.—330 C.E.:
Apostolic, Apologist and Church Fathers © 2013 by
Christian Publishing House

Christian Publishing House,
support@christianpublishers.org

Senior Editor: Edward D. Andrews
Managing Editor: Bruce Prince
Copy Editor: Edward D. Andrews
Cover and Page Design: Edward D. Andrews

Christian Publishing House

Professional Christian Publishing of the Good News

Preface

In the beginning of the second century C.E., false teachings had arisen to twist the Christian truth of Jesus and the apostles of the first century. Christian Publishing House has given us a look into Early Christianity, by way of Apostolic, Apologist, and Church Fathers. These men's writings and example deliver an insight into the religious environment of their day. The apologists defended the teachings and practices of orthodox Christians. Moreover, for professing true Christianity, many were put to death rather than deny Jesus Christ. Particularly striking was their love for truth and their bold witnessing in spite of the persecution.

Between the delightfully illustrated covers, Christian Publishing House has presented fourteen Apostolic, Apologist and Church Fathers from Polycarp, a student of the apostle John in the late first century, to Jerome in the fourth century. It is to these eminent scholars, whose occupations covered all walks of life: shepherd, mathematician, lawyer, and bishop, that we owe, among other things, the divine compilation of our Bible canon today. We are so fortunate to have the teachings of these eminent scholars whose writings have been of interest to genuine Christians throughout the last 2,000 years, as well as in our modern age.—Bruce Prince.

CHAPTER 1 Clement of Rome - Apostolic Father

Scott Korljan

Clement of Rome belongs to a group of early church leaders that have been known since the seventeenth century as the "Apostolic Fathers." This title signifies the fact that these men, most of who lived in the second half of the first century and the first half of the second century, were the first generation of church leaders after the original apostles. As such, many of these leaders had personal contact of some sort with the original twelve. So, if you have ever wondered what conditions were like in the early church immediately after the apostolic age, these are the men that you want to get to know.

Identified by some as the Clement to which the apostle Paul referred to as his fellow laborer in Phil 4:3, Clement of Rome is an important figure in church history and one of the earliest Apostolic Fathers. Although very little is known about the details of his life, he has been officially declared a "saint" and is celebrated on November 23rd in the Roman Catholic, Anglican, and Lutheran Churches. His letter to the Corinthian Church is one of the earliest surviving Christian documents outside of the New Testament and provides insight into early church practice and teaching.

Early Life and History

We have very little information about the life of Clement other than the fact that he served as Bishop of the Church at Rome. Much of what we know about his

9

time as Bishop was recorded by Christian leader Irenaeus almost a full century after Clements death. "The blessed Apostles, Peter and Paul, having built up the Church of Rome, entrusted the bishopric to Linus, who was followed by Anacletus, and third in succession to the Apostles Clement obtained the bishopric; who had also himself seen the blessed Apostles, and had conferred with them, and had still their preaching sounding in his ears, and their traditions before his eyes; not alone, for there were still many left of those who had been taught by the Apostles. In the time of this Clement, no small dissension arising among the brethren at Corinth, the Church at Rome sent a very weighty epistle to the Corinthians reconciling them to peace, and restoring their faith, and declaring to them the traditions they had recently received from the Apostles."[1]

From this statement we learn that Clement served as the bishop of the church at Rome, during which time he authored a letter to the church at Corinth. Historians have fixed the date of his bishopric at Rome as lasting from roughly 92 to 101 AD.[2] Nothing is known about his later life or death. Some later Christian writers believed he was martyred for the faith, and there is a legend that developed about him being imprisoned under the Roman Emperor Trajan and tied to an anchor and thrown into

[1] As quoted in Ernest Leigh-Bennett, *Handbook of the Early Christian Fathers*, (London: Williams and Norgate, 1920), 1.

[2] Ibid. These dates are based on the above statement by Irenaeus as well as other references to Clement in ancient writings from historians such as Jerome and Eusebius.

the Black Sea. There is no reliable evidence to substantiate such a claim, however.[3]

Historical Setting

Clement was leader to the church in Rome, the capital of the ancient world. The Roman church is most well-known to Christians today because of the Apostle Paul's famous letter which is now contained in the New Testament. Although Irenaeus claimed that the Roman Church was founded by Peter and Paul (See above quote), it is more likely that Christianity spread to Rome by Jews converted on the day of Pentecost.[4] Christians living in Rome often faced difficult circumstances and persecution in the first several centuries. As early as 49 A.D. there is documented evidence that the emperor Claudius "expelled all of the Jews from Rome because they were constantly rioting at the instigation of Chrestus."[5] Then, under emperor Nero 64 A.D., persecution against Christians broke out again. According to the Roman historian Tacitus, Nero attempted to shift the blame for a devastating fire which destroyed much of the city onto Christians after a rumor began that he had started the fire. It was probably during Nero's persecutions that the Apostles Peter and Paul were

---

[3] The oldest and most reliable sources for Clement do not contain any indication that he was martyred.

[4] For a more in depth discussion of why Peter and Paul were unlikely to have founded the church at Rome, see D.A. Carson, Douglass Moo, and Leon Morris, An Introduction to the New Testament, (Grand Rapids: Zondervan, 1992), 242.

[5] Ibid, 243. As Carson and Moo note, the Romans at this early stage would not have distinguished between Jews and Jewish Christians, so the expulsion would have included them both.

martyred. Persecutions also occurred under the Emperor Domitian at the end of the 1st century. It was during these persecutions that the Apostle John was exiled to the Isle of Patmos, where he wrote the book of Revelation. The reasons for these persecutions varied, but many times involved the Christians refusal to worship the emperor as God, as Domitian and other emperors demanded.

Serving as the Bishop of Rome in the last decade of the 1st century, Clement was leading the church during the Domitian persecutions. His initial statement in his letter to the Corinthian church hints at the difficulties that the church in Rome was facing during his leadership: "Owing to the suddenly bursting and rapidly succeeding calamities and untoward experiences that have befallen us, we have been somewhat tardy, we think, in giving our attention to the subjects of dispute in your community, beloved."[6]

Writings

The only undisputed writing that has come down to us from Clement is his epistle to the Corinthian church. This letter was quite lengthy, about two times the size of the book of Hebrews, and was occasioned by a schism in the church at Corinth. Specifically, it appears that several members of the Corinthian church had undermined and removed several elders from leadership, creating factions and a large controversy in the Church. Clement wrote his letter for the purpose of restoring order.

---

[6] First Epistle of Clement to the Corinthians, as contained in Johannes Quasten and Joseph Plumpe, editors, *Ancient Christians Writers: The Works of the Fathers in Translation*, (New York: Newman Press, 1946), 9.

The letter can be divided into two main parts, the first section providing a more general treatment of how Christians ought to conduct themselves, and the second dealing more specifically with the disruption within the Corinthian church.[7] The first section involves heavy quotation from the Old Testament to demonstrate how conflict and disturbances in the past were ordinarily due to "jealousy and envy" and that God's blessing come upon those who make peace and submit to proper authority. The second section stresses the need for a submissive attitude and spirit, and calls upon the leaders of the schism to repent.[8] Also noteworthy about this letter, as it addresses the need for proper submission to church authority, is the lack of reference to a single ruling bishop. As the bishop of Rome, Clement does not assume to himself any special authority over other church leaders, and refers to church leaders as either bishops and deacons or elders. In other words, there is no evidence of the idea of the papacy found in this early writing.

Other writings have been attributed to Clement, most notably a second letter to the Corinthian church. However, the consensus of most scholars today is that Clement did not author any of them. The second letter was an anonymous sermon, but it is now believed to have been written too late to have been by Clement. Other later documents, such as two letters on Virginity,

---

[7] Ibid, 5. I am following the division suggested by the editors as a good way to summarize the contents of the letter. For more details, see pages 5-6.

[8] Ibid.

are other works formerly attributed to Clement, which are now regarded as spurious.[9]

Teaching

The only source that we have by which to ascertain Clements teaching and doctrine is his letter to the Corinthian Church. This makes analysis of his theology tricky, as the letter was written as a pastoral admonition and not as a theological treatise. However, we can get a glimpse of his teaching on some of the core doctrines of Christianity.

God. -- Clement had a high view of God's sovereignty and power, which comes out in various ways in his letter. God is called "the great Framer and Lord of all," "the Almighty," "the All-seeing," "He comprehends all things," He knows all of the thoughts and intentions of men, etc.[10]

Christ. -- Clement had high regard for both the person and work of Christ. He called Jesus "Lord" throughout the letter, such as in the salutation: "The Church of god which resides...at Rome to the Church of God which is a stranger at Corinth; to those who are called and sanctified by the will of God through our Lord Jesus Christ. May grace and peace from Almighty God flow to you in rich profusion through Jesus Christ!" Although Clement does not fully expound his understanding of Christ's work of atonement, he does clearly believe that Christ died for our sins: "Let us

---

[9] For further discussion, see James Donaldson, *A Critical History of Christian Literature and Doctrine* (vol 1), (London: Macmillan and Co, 1864), 119.

[10] For a more complete list, see Donaldson pages 123ff.

reverences the Lord Jesus Christ, whose blood was given for us," "On account of the love which He had to us, Jesus Christ our Lord gave his blood for us by the will of God, even flesh for our flesh and soul for our souls."[11]

Trinity. -- The doctrine of the Trinity would not come to full fruition for several centuries, but the seeds can already be found in Clements letter. In place of the more Jewish "As the Lord Jehovah liveth," Clement used "As God liveth and Jesus Christ liveth, and the Holy Spirit, who are the hope and faith of the elect."[12]

Salvation. -- Salvation is tied very closely to good works, much as James does in his epistle. The letter contains very little reference to or discussion of faith in Christ, and much on the need for good works. However, Clement seems to have believed in salvation by faith, writing: "We are declared and made righteous, not by means of ourselves, nor through our own wisdom or understanding or piety or works which we did in holiness of heart, but through faith."[13]

Future State. -- Clement gives much attention to the resurrection of the body, even using some of Paul's analogy from 1 Cor 15. Those who die in Christ go to "the place of glory that is due." Christ will come again in the future.

The Scripture. -- One of the characteristics of his letter is the frequent quotation of Scripture, especially from the Old Testament. He most heavily mentions and uses Moses, David, Isaiah, Jeremiah, and Ezekiel. He has

---

[11] Ibid. 124-130.

[12] Leigh-Bennett, *Handbook*, 6.

[13] Donaldson, *A Critical History*, 133.

a high view of the authority of the Scripture, believing that prophets spoke by the Holy Spirit: "Examine carefully the Scriptures, the true (sayings) of the Holy Spirit;" "The servants of the grace of God spoke through the Holy Spirit..." Clement also referenced the New Testament letter of 1 Corinthians, the teaching of Jesus from the Sermon on the Mount, and echoes many of the themes found in Paul, Peter, James, and the first three Gospels.[14]

Conclusion

Although our knowledge of Clement is limited, he nevertheless has an important place in Church history as one of the earliest leaders of the post-apostolic Church. His letter to the Corinthians was highly valued by the early church, and provides Christians today with a peak into the life and practice of the early church.

---

[14] Ibid, 144-150.

CHAPTER 2 Ignatius of Antioch - Early Christian Writings

CHAPTER 2 Ignatius of Antioch, also known as (ca. 35 or 50) - (from 98 to 117)[15] was among the Apostolic Fathers, was the third Bishop of Antioch, and was a student of John the Apostle.[16] En route to Rome, where according to Christian tradition, he met his martyrdom, he wrote a series of letters which have been preserved as an example of very early Christian theology. Important topics addressed in these letters include ecclesiology, the sacraments, and the role of bishops.

Early Life and Ministry

Ignatius converted to Christianity at a young age.[17] Later in his life he was chosen to serve as the Bishop of Antioch, succeeding Saint Peter and St. Evodius (who died around A.D. 67). The fourth century Church historian Eusebius records that Ignatius succeeded Evodius.[18] Making his apostolic succession even more immediate, Theodoret of Cyrrhus reported that St. Peter himself appointed Ignatius to the episcopal see of Antioch.[19] Ignatius called himself Theophorus (God

---

[15] http://en.wikipedia.org/wiki/Ignatius_of_Antioch

[16] The Martyrdom of Ignatius / Synaxarium: The Martyrdom of St. Ignatius, Patriarch of Antioch

[17] AmericanCatholic.org "St. Ignatius of Antioch

[18] Historia Ecclesiastica, II.iii.22.

[19] Dial. Immutab., I, iv, 33a.

Bearer). A tradition arose that he was one of the children whom Jesus took in his arms and blessed.[20]

Ignatius is one of the five Apostolic Fathers (the earliest authoritative group of the Church Fathers). He based his authority on being a bishop of the Church, living his life in the imitation of Christ. It is believed that St. Ignatius, along with his friend Polycarp, with great probability were disciples of the Apostle St. John.[21]

Rome Epistles attributed to Ignatius report his arrest by the authorities and travel to Rome:

From Syria even to Rome I fight with wild beasts, by land and sea, by night and by day, being bound amidst ten leopards, even a company of soldiers, who only grow worse when they are kindly treated. — Ignatius to the Romans.[22]

Along the route he wrote six letters to the churches in the region and one to a fellow bishop. According to Christian legend, he was sentenced to die at the Colosseum.[23] In his Chronicle, Eusebius gives the date of Ignatius's death as AA 2124 (2124 years after Adam), which would amount to the 11th year of Trajan's reign; i.e., A.D. 108.[24]

According to Christian legend,after Ignatius' martyrdom in the Colosseum, his remains were carried back to Antioch by his companions and were interred

---

[20] The Martyrdom of Ignatius

[21] St. Ignatius in Antioch profile at NewAdvent.org

[22] Historia Ecclesiastica, II.iii.22.

[23] St. Ignatius of Antioch profile at EWTN website

[24] Chronicle, from the Latin translation of Jerome, p. 276.

outside the city gates. The reputed remains of Ignatius were moved by the Emperor Theodosius II to the Tychaeum, or Temple of Tyche, which had been converted into a church dedicated to Ignatius. In 637 the relics were transferred to the Basilica di San Clemente in Rome.

Veneration

Ignatius' feast day is observed on 20 December in the Eastern Orthodox Church. In the Coptic Orthodox Church of Alexandria, he is commemorated, according to its Synaxarium, on the 24th of the Coptic Month of Kiahk (which currently falls on January 2, but is equivalent to December 20 in the Gregorian Calendar due to the current 13-day Julian-Gregorian Calendar offset).In the Syriac Orthodox Church and Indian Orthodox Church,which also follows Syriac rites, his feast is observed on the 20th of December. His celebration is on 1 February in the General Roman Calendar of 1962.

Today Western Christianity follows the Syriac churches in keeping his feast on 17 October.[25]

Letters

The seven letters considered to be authentic are[citation needed]

- To the Ephesians,
- To the Magnesians,
- Letter to the Trallians,
- To the Romans,

---

[25] Calendarium Romanum (Vatican City, 1969).

- To the Philadelphians,
- To the Smyrnaeans,
- To Polycarp, Bishop of Smyrna.

By the 5th century, this authentic collection had been enlarged by spurious letters, and some of the original letters had been changed with interpolations, created to posthumously enlist Ignatius as an unwitting witness in theological disputes of that age, while the purported eye-witness account of his martyrdom is also thought to be a forgery from around the same time. A detailed but spurious account of Ignatius' arrest and his travails and martyrdom is the material of the Martyrium Ignatii which is presented as being an eyewitness account for the church of Antioch, and as if written by Ignatius' companions, Philo of Cilicia, deacon at Tarsus, and Rheus Agathopus, a Syrian.

Although James Ussher regarded it as genuine, if there is any genuine nucleus of the Martyrium, it has been so greatly expanded with interpolations that no part of it is without questions. Its most reliable manuscript is the 10th century Codex Colbertinus (Paris), in which the Martyrium closes the collection. The Martyrium presents the confrontation of the bishop Ignatius with Trajan at Antioch, a familiar trope of Acta of the martyrs, and many details of the long, partly overland voyage to Rome. The Synaxarium of the Coptic Orthodox Church of Alexandria says that he was thrown to the wild beasts that devoured him and rent him to pieces.[26]

Ignatius's letters proved to be important testimony to the development of Christian theology, since the

---

[26] Synaxarium: The Martyrdom of St. Ignatius, Patriarch of Antioch

number of extant writings from this period of Church history is very small. They bear signs of being written in great haste and without a proper plan, such as run-on sentences and an unsystematic succession of thought. Ignatius is the earliest known Christian writer to emphasize loyalty to a single bishop in each city (or diocese) who is assisted by both presbyters possibly elders and deacons. Earlier writings only mention either bishops or presbyters, and give the impression that there was usually more than one bishop per congregation. Philippians 1:1

For instance, while the offices of bishop, presbyter, and deacon appear apostolic in origin, the titles of "bishop" and "presbyter" could be used interchangeably:

> Take care to do all things in harmony with God, with the bishop presiding in the place of God, and with the presbyters in the place of the council of the apostles, and with the deacons, who are most dear to me, entrusted with the business of Jesus Christ, who was with the Father from the beginning and is at last made manifest — Letter to the Magnesians 2, 6:1

Ignatius is known to have taught the deity of Christ:

> There is one Physician who is possessed both of flesh and spirit; both made and not made; God existing in flesh; true life in death; both of Mary and of God; first passible and then impassible, even Jesus Christ our Lord. — Letter to the Ephesians, ch. 7, shorter version, Roberts-Donaldson translation

He stressed the value of the Eucharist, calling it a "medicine of immortality" (Ignatius to the Ephesians

20:2). The very strong desire for bloody martyrdom in the arena, which Ignatius expresses rather graphically in places, may seem quite odd to the modern reader. An examination of his theology of soteriology shows that he regarded salvation as one being free from the powerful fear of death and thus to bravely face martyrdom.[27] Ignatius is claimed to be the first known Christian writer to argue in favor of Christianity's replacement of the Sabbath with the Lord's Day:

> Be not seduced by strange doctrines nor by antiquated fables, which are profitless. For if even unto this day we live after the manner of Judaism, we avow that we have not received grace.... If then those who had walked in ancient practices attained unto newness of hope, no longer observing Sabbaths but fashioning their lives after the Lord's day, on which our life also arose through Him and through His death which some men deny ... how shall we be able to live apart from Him? ... It is monstrous to talk of Jesus Christ and to practise Judaism. For Christianity did not believe in Judaism, but Judaism in Christianity — Ignatius to the Magnesians 8:1, 9:1-2, 10:3, Lightfoot translation.

He is also responsible for the first known use of the Greek word *katholikos*, meaning "universal", "complete" and "whole" to describe the church, writing:

> Wherever the bishop appears, there let the people be; as wherever Jesus Christ is, there is the Catholic Church. It is not lawful to baptize

---

[27] L. Stephanie Cobb, Dying To Be Men: Gender and Language in Early Christian Martyr Texts, page 3 (Columbia University Press, 2008);

or give communion without the consent of the bishop. On the other hand, whatever has his approval is pleasing to God. Thus, whatever is done will be safe and valid. — Letter to the Smyrnaeans 8, J.R. Willis translation.

It is from the word katholikos ("according to the whole") that the word catholic comes. When Ignatius wrote the Letter to the Smyrnaeans in about the year 107 and used the word catholic, he used it as if it were a word already in use to describe the Church. This has led many scholars to conclude that the appellation Catholic Church with its ecclesial connotation may have been in use as early as the last quarter of the 1st century. On the Eucharist, he wrote in his letter to the Smyrnaeans:

> Take note of those who hold heterodox opinions on the grace of Jesus Christ which has come to us, and see how contrary their opinions are to the mind of God ... They abstain from the Eucharist and from prayer because they do not confess that the Eucharist is the flesh of our Savior Jesus Christ, flesh which suffered for our sins and which that Father, in his goodness, raised up again. They who deny the gift of God are perishing in their disputes. — Letter to the Smyrnaeans 6:2–7:1

Ignatius modeled his writings after Paul, Peter, and John, and even quoted or paraphrased their own works freely, such as when he quoted 1 Cor 1:18, in his letter to the Ephesians:[28]

> Let my spirit be counted as nothing for the sake of the cross, which is a stumbling-block to

---

[28] Byfield, Ted, ed. A Pinch on Incense, pg 50

those that do not believe, but to us salvation and life eternal. - Letter to the Ephesians 18, Roberts and Donaldson translation

Saint Ignatius's most famous quotation, however, comes from his letter to the Romans:

I am writing to all the Churches and I enjoin all, that I am dying willingly for God's sake, if only you do not prevent it. I beg you, do not do me an untimely kindness. Allow me to be eaten by the beasts, which are my way of reaching to God. I am God's wheat, and I am to be ground by the teeth of wild beasts, so that I may become the pure bread of Christ. — Letter to the Romans

CHAPTER 3 Polycarp of Smyrna - A Disciple of John

Edward D. Andrews

The thousands, who surrounded him in the arena, viewed him as a godless man, who was causing their countrymen to abandon their worship, believing that this man worked toward the destruction of their gods. The crowd's stares were of malicious hatred, as they despised his very presence. The governor called him forward; this dignified man of 86 years of age stepped into the open and acknowledged his identity. His name was Polycarp.

Figure 1 http://ancientwordtour.wordpress.com

But as Polycarp entered the stadium, there came a voice from heaven: "Be strong, Polycarp, and act like a man." And no one saw the speaker, but those of our people who were present heard the voice. And then, as he was brought forward, there was a great tumult when they heard that Polycarp had been arrested. (2) Therefore, when he was brought before him, the proconsul asked if he were Polycarp.[29] And when he confessed that he was, the proconsul tried to persuade him to recant, saying, "Have respect for your age," and other such things as they are accustomed to say: "Swear by the Genius[30] of Caesar; repent; say, 'Away with the atheists!' " So Polycarp solemnly looked at the whole crowd of lawless heathen who were in the stadium, motioned toward them with his hand, and then (groaning as he looked up to heaven) said, "Away with the atheists!" (3) But when the magistrate persisted and said, "Swear the oath, and I will release you; revile Christ," Polycarp replied, "For eighty-six years I have been his servant,[31] and he has done me no wrong. How can I blaspheme my King who saved me?"[32]

You are the reader are likely asking why is the 86 year old man on trial? Who exactly was Polycarp? And what was it that brought him to this point in his life?

---

[29] *Polycarp*: so gE; m (followed by Lightfoot) omits.

[30] Genius: i.e., the guardian spirit.

[31] *have ... servant*: so g; mE read *have served him*.

[32] Michael William Holmes, *The Apostolic Fathers: Greek Texts and English Translations*, Third ed. (Grand Rapids, Mich.: Baker Books, 2007), 315, 317.

Early Life and Ministry

Polycarp was born to Christian parents about 69 C.E. in Asia Minor, at Smyrna. As he grew into a man, he was known for his kindness, self-discipline, compassionate treatment of others, and thorough study of God's Word. Soon enough he became an elder in the Christian congregation at Smyrna.

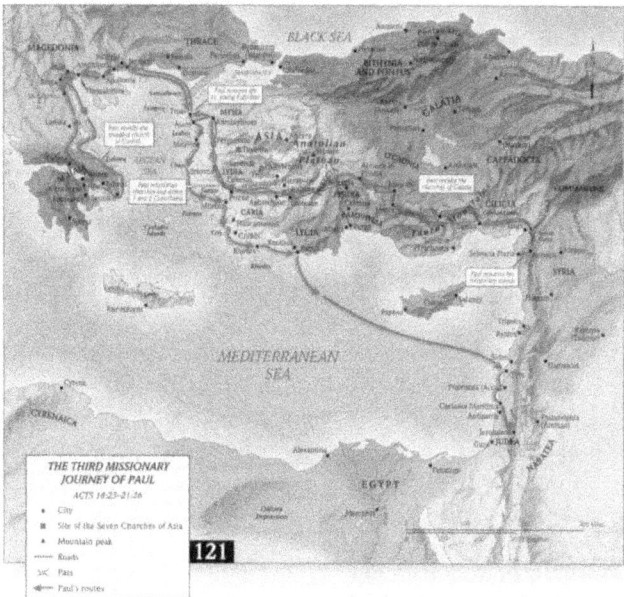

Figure 2 Third Missionary Journey of Paul Courtesy of Access Foundation

Polycarp was very fortunate to live in a time, where he was able to learn from the apostles themselves. In fact, the apostle John was one of his teachers. Listen to Irenaeus'[33] own words about Polycarp:

> Polycarp was not only instructed by apostles and conversant with many who had seen the Lord, but was appointed by apostles to serve in Asia as Bishop of Smyrna. I myself saw him in my early years, for he lived a long time and was very old indeed when he laid down his life by a glorious and most splendid martyrdom. At all times he taught the things which he had learnt from the apostles, which the Church transmits, which alone are true. These facts are attested by all the churches of Asia and the successors of Polycarp to this day—and he was a much more trustworthy and dependable witness to the truth than Valentinus and Marcion and all other wrong-headed persons. In the time of Anicetus he stayed for a while in Rome, where he won over many from the camp of these heretics in the Church of God, proclaiming that the one and only truth he had received from the apostles was the truth transmitted by the Church. And there are people who heard him describe how John, the Lord's disciple, when at Ephesus went to take a bath, but seeing Cerinthus inside rushed out of the building without taking a bath, crying: "Let us get out of here, for fear the place falls in, now that

---

[33] Irenaeus was born between 120 C.E. and 140 C.E. in or near the city of Smyrna, who died about 200 C.E. He served as an elder in Gaul. He was an early apologist, who wrote in defense of the Christian truth as he knew it. His principal writing was *The Refutation and Overthrow of the Knowledge Falsely So Called*," which was commonly referred to as "*Against Heresies*."

Cerinthus, the enemy of the truth, is inside!" Polycarp himself on one occasion came face to face with Marcion, and when Marcion said "Don't you recognize me?" he replied: "I do indeed: I recognize the firstborn of Satan!" So careful were the apostles and their disciples to avoid even exchanging words with any falsifier of the truth, in obedience to the Pauline injunction: "If a man remains heretical after more than one warning, have no more to do with him, recognizing that a person of that type is a perverted sinner, self–condemned.[34]

A Witness to the Truth

It is very fortunate that Polycarp received the training that he did, from the apostles, especially John. He was entering the beginning of the time period of the foretold apostasy [rebellion, falling away]:

2 Thessalonians 2:1-3 New American Standard Bible (NASB)

[1] Now we request you, brethren, with regard to the coming of our Lord Jesus Christ and our gathering together to Him, [2] that you not be quickly shaken from your composure or be disturbed either by a spirit or a message or a letter as if from us, to the effect that the day of the Lord has come. [3] Let no one in any way deceive you, for **it will not come unless the apostasy [rebellion, falling away] comes first**, and the man of lawlessness is revealed, the son of destruction.

---

[34] Irenaeus Against Heresies 3.3.4; Eusebius, Ecclesiastical History 4.14.3–8. This translation from edition cited above.

Polycarp was often moved to go out of his way to be there for others. For example, when Ignatius of Antioch, Syria, on the way to his martyrdom in Rome, asked the Philippians to send a letter to his congregation, Polycarp of Smyrna made sure it was delivered.

In Polycarp's letter to the Philippians, we can appreciate the truths he shares with his readers.

I greatly rejoice with you in our Lord Jesus Christ, because you welcomed the representations of the true love[35] and, as was proper for you, helped on their way those men confined by chains suitable for saints, which are the diadems of those who are truly chosen by God and our Lord; (2) and because your firmly rooted faith, renowned from the earliest times, still perseveres and bears fruit to our Lord Jesus Christ, who endured for our sins, facing even death, "whom God raised up, having loosed the pangs of Hades." (3) "Though you have not seen him, you believe in him with an inexpressible and glorious joy" (which many desire to experience), knowing that "by grace you have been saved, not because of works," but by the will of God through Jesus Christ.

"Therefore prepare for action and serve God in fear" and truth, leaving behind the empty and meaningless talk and the error of the crowd, and "believing in him who raised" our Lord Jesus Christ "from the dead and gave him glory" and a throne at his right hand; to whom all things in heaven and on earth were subjected, whom every breathing creature

---

[35] I.e., Ignatius and his companions.

serves, who is coming as "Judge of the living and the dead," for whose blood God will hold responsible those who disobey him. (2) But "he who raised him from the dead will raise us also," if we do his will and follow his commandments and love the things he loved, while avoiding every kind of unrighteousness, greed, love of money, slander and false testimony; "not repaying evil for evil or insult for insult" or blow for blow or curse for curse, (3) but instead remembering what the Lord said as he taught: "Do not judge, that you may not be judged; forgive, and you will be forgiven; show mercy, that you may be shown mercy; with the measure you use, it will be measured back to you"; and "blessed are the poor and those who are persecuted for righteousness' sake, for theirs is the kingdom of God."[36]—Luke 6:20 and Matt. 5:10; cf. Matt. 5:3.

As you can see from the footnotes Polycarp quoted abundantly from the Scriptures. In his letter to the Philippians, he referred to Matthew, Acts, Romans, 1 Corinthians, 2 Corinthians, Galatians, Ephesians, 2 Thessalonians, 1 Timothy, 1 Peter, to mention just a few. This sets a good example for us to follow, and should help us to appreciate that the apologist, who lived right after the death of the last apostle, John; used the Scriptures to defend the truth as they understood it.

---

[36] Michael William Holmes, The Apostolic Fathers: Greek Texts and English Translations, Updated ed. (Grand Rapids, Mich.: Baker Books, 2007), 281, 283.

Polycarp in Smyrna

Figure 3 http://www.wildwinds.com/coins/sear5/s3526

Smyrna was an ancient coastal city of Asia Minor, on the Aegean shore of what is now Asiatic Turkey. It was full of activity and a flourishing trading center. It had a temple of Tiberius Caesar and so sponsored emperor worship. In addition, Roman emperors were presented importantly as deities on coins and in inscriptions. Pagan religious philosophies were endorsed by royal authority.

Regardless of the wealth that was flowing into Smyrna, many of those within the Christian congregation were materially poor. However, in the time of the apostle John (c. 96 C.E.), they were commended for being spiritually rich.

Revelation 2:8-10 English Standard Version (ESV)

[8] "And to the angel of the church in Smyrna write: 'The words of the first and the last, who died and came to life.

⁹ "'I know your tribulation and your poverty (but you are rich) and the slander of those who say that they are Jews and are not, but are a synagogue of Satan. **¹⁰** Do not fear what you are about to suffer. Behold, the devil is about to throw some of you into prison, that you may be tested, and for ten days you will have tribulation. Be faithful unto death, and I will give you the crown of life.

Figure 4 http://thetathreads.com

We can attribute this spiritual maturity among the Christians in Smyrna, to the hard work of the elders, like Polycarp. Throughout the time of Polycarp's serving as oversight in the congregation, these ones lived through one difficult religious struggle after another. There was the pressure from the Roman government, the fleshly non-Christian Jews, as well as conflicting creeds and cults. The community that they had to go into, to spread the gospel, was widespread with demonic practices, such as sorcery and astrology, and thus the atmosphere was one of godlessness. The martyrdom of Polycarp took place on February 23, 155 C.E., where extremist Jews apparently helped with the gathering of firewood. They did this even though the execution took place on a great Sabbath day!

The Godless

After withdrawing from the city, Polycarp is hunted by a police captain named Herod and betrayed by young slaves who belong to his own house (6:2). He is arrested late in the evening in an "upper room" by police armed as if advancing against a robber (7:1; cf. Mt. 26:55). He refuses to flee, but like Jesus in Gethsemane says "the will of God be done." After a long prayer (7:3) he is taken back to the city riding on an ass on a "great Sabbath day" (8:1).[37]

Back in the arena, Polycarp was standing before the governor and an enormous crowd, looking for blood. The governor continued to push him to profess worshipful honor to Caesar:

But as he continued to insist, saying, "Swear by the Genius of Caesar," he answered: "If you vainly suppose that I will swear by the Genius of Caesar, as you request, and pretend not to know who I am, listen carefully: I am a Christian. Now if you want to learn the

---

[37] Geoffrey W. Bromiley, vol. 1, *The International Standard Bible Encyclopedia, Revised* (Wm. B. Eerdmans, 1988; 2002), 211.

doctrine of Christianity, name a day and give me a hearing." (2) The proconsul said: "Persuade the people." But Polycarp said: "You I might have considered worthy of a reply, for we have been taught to pay proper respect to rulers and authorities appointed by God, as long as it does us no harm; but as for these, I do not think they are worthy, that I should have to defend myself before them."[38]

Just moments later Polycarp was burned to death because he would not forsake Jesus Christ.

---

[38] Michael William Holmes, *The Apostolic Fathers: Greek Texts and English Translations*, Third ed. (Grand Rapids, Mich.: Baker Books, 2007), 315, 317.

CHAPTER 4 Barnabas - The Anonymous Teacher

Bruce Prince

The world is generally aware of only two people from ancient times with the name of Barnabas. First, there was the friend and traveling companion of Paul in the first century and a cousin of Mark the Gospel writer. The other was an unknown Alexandrian Jew in the times of Trajan and Hadrian of the second-century C.E.[39] who wrote a twenty-one chapter epistle. The reason for localizing the epistle's origins to Alexandria is that up to the fourth century only the Alexandrian Christians were acquainted with the epistle, and it attained in their church the honour of being publicly read.[40]

The Church of Rome ascribed the epistle to the former Barnabas, friend and companion of the Apostle Paul, because they believed that he was the author of our biblical book Hebrews, and the epistle "has his style", so they believed.[41] However, even though our New Testament Barnabas did not write the epistle ascribed to his name, the letter has become known as the Epistle of Barnabas. The writer's name may, or may not have been Barnabas, but because the epistle that he wrote has become known as the "Epistle of Barnabas", this anonymous teacher has been generally given the name

---

[39] Ante-Nicene Fathers, Roberts & Donaldson, Vol.1

[40] The Catholic Encyclopedia. New York: Robert Appleton Company. Retrieved May 11, 2013 from New Advent: http://www.newadvent.org/cathen/02299a.htm

[41] http://www.ccel.org/ccel/schaff/anf01.vi.i.html

"Barnabas" down through the ages, even though that may not have been the author's real name. It will be observed in his "Epistle" that he nowhere claims to be the apostle Barnabas; indeed his language is such as to suggest that he was wholly unconnected with the apostles.[42]

The Epistle of Barnabas is sometimes found in the canonical listing of New Testament books. Origen quotes it as Scripture in his "Commentary on Romans" (1.18), but apostolic fathers, Eusebius and Jerome regarded the letter as non-canonical. Subsequent history demonstrated that it ultimately was not considered as part of the New Testament Scriptures. The Codex Sinaiticus[43], however, included the epistle among what was considered the canonical books at that time. Today however, scholars commonly consider the epistle a pseudepigrapha[44] work, composed by a Gentile Christian of Alexandria rather than by the Barnabas mentioned in the New Testament.[45] The manner in which Clement of Alexandria refers to the letter gives confirmation to the belief that by about the year 200 C.E., even in Alexandria, not everyone regarded the Epistle of Barnabas as an inspired writing.[46]

---

[42] "The Apostolic Fathers", J.B. Lightfoot p240

[43] "Codex Sinaiticus" literally means "the Sinai book" – a Greek hand-written document dating from the fourth century and discovered by students in a Greek Orthodox Monastery in the 19th century. Apart from the Epistle of Barnabas, it contains all the NT books as we have them today, but in a slightly different order, as well as all books of the OT.

[44] Pseudepigrapha were anonymous or pseudonymous writings professing to be biblical, but not included in any biblical canon

[45] Myers, A. C. (1987). *The Eerdmans Bible dictionary* (126). Grand Rapids, MI: Eerdmans.

[46] Catholic Encyclopedia 1907

Early Life and Ministry

Little is known of this writer of the second century. Historians are not even sure of his real name. It appears he was basically a layman because of the number of Scriptural errors in his writings, and it is believed he was an Alexandrian Jew in the times of Trajan and Hadrian[47] of the second century.[48] We know nothing certain of the region where the author lived, or where his first readers were to be found. The epistle does not give enough indications to permit confident identification of either the teacher's location or the region to which he writes. His thought, hermeneutical methods, and style have many parallels throughout the known Jewish and Christian worlds. Most scholars have located the work's origin in the area of Alexandria, because it has many affinities with Alexandrian Jewish and Christian thought and because its first witnesses are Alexandrian. Recently, Prigent (Prigent and Kraft 1971: 20-24), Wengst (1971: 114-18), and Scorza Barcellona (1975: 62-65) have suggested other origins based on affinities in Palestine, Syria, and Asia Minor. The place of origin must remain an open question, although the Greek-speaking Eastern Mediterranean appears most probable.[49]

The intention of the writer, as he himself states in the first chapter of his epistle, was "to perfect the knowledge" of those to whom he wrote. Although the

---

[47] Roman Emperors in the second century.

[48] Ante-Nicene Fathers, Roberts & Donaldson, Vol.1

[49] Jay Curry (*The Anchor Bible Dictionary*, v. 1, pp. 613-614)

work is not gnostic[50] in a theological sense, the author, who considers himself to be a teacher to the unidentified audience to which he writes (see e.g. 9.9), intends to impart to his readers the perfect gnosis (special knowledge), that they may perceive that the Christians, as opposed to the Jews, are God's only true covenant people.[51]

Hilgenfeld, who has devoted much attention to this epistle, holds that it was written toward the close of the first century at the Gentile Christian School of Alexandria, with the view of winning back, or guarding from a Judaic form of Christianity, those Christians belonging to the same class as himself."[52] The *raison d'etre* of the document appears therefore, to be the author's fear that some members of this group are being swayed by teachings, which emphasize the lasting quality of the Jewish Covenant with God. Much of the document, therefore, is taken up with dismantling this idea.[53] Barnabas is thus an early example of an early Christian writer trying to distance Christians from Judaism. Its existence is a window into the kinds of teachings that might have been circulating amongst Christians of the second century.

---

[50] Gnosticism relates to special mystical knowledge, especially knowledge of so-called spiritual truths of deep things unknown to everyday Christians.

[51] Kraft, Robert A., Barnabas and the Didache: Volume 3 of The Apostolic Fathers: A New Translation and Commentary, edited by Robert Grant. New York: Thomas Nelson and Sons, 1965

[52] "The Ante-Nicene Fathers", Roberts & Donaldson, Vol 1, Buffalo: The Christian Literature Company 1885. Introductory Note to the Epistle of Barnabas.

[53] Ecole Initiative – an attempt to create a hypertext encyclopedia of early Christian church history on the Web.

In the epistle, there is a dividing into them and us: us being the Christians and them being Jews, us being in, them being out. Barnabas is unambiguous about the fate of the Covenant at Sinai and sees no room for two competing covenants. There is one covenant and it belongs to the Christians. Moreover, the Temple and all the commandments are not to be interpreted literally. On every other point of exegesis the worst that could be inferred about the Jewish understanding of the Covenant or of Jewish ritual and practices is that they are misguided or misinterpreted. There are no accusations of deicide (death of a god), the Law is not condemned as inherently evil or imposed on the Jewish people to curb idolatry. Although it is idolatry that causes the covenant to be destroyed, Barnabas makes no effort to extend the accusation beyond Sinai. Barnabas is far more concerned with combating the idea of dual covenants (an idea unlikely to have been generated from within Jewish circles).[54]

Historical Setting

The date, object, and intended reader of the epistle can only be doubtfully inferred from some statements that it contains. It was clearly written after the destruction of Jerusalem, since reference is made to that event, but how long after is a matter of much dispute. In chapter 16, verses 3 & 4, the Epistle reads:

> Furthermore he says again, 'Behold, those who tore down this temple will themselves

---

[54] Edwards, Mark (1995): "Ignatius, Judaism, and Judaizing" Eranos 93, 69-77

build it.' It is happening. For because of their fighting it was torn down by the enemies. And now the very servants of the enemies will themselves rebuild it.

This passage clearly places the date of the epistle after the destruction of the Second Temple in 70 C.E. However, it also places it before the Bar Kochba Revolt of 132 C.E., after which there could have been no hope that the Romans would help to rebuild the temple. The document must come from the period between the two revolts.[55] The rebuilding referred to may have reference to the building in Hadrian's time (117-138 C.E.) of a pagan temple on the site of the destroyed Herod's temple, and the date of writing is probably therefore, about 130-132 C.E.[56]

Up until 1843, eight manuscripts of the Epistle of Barnabas were known to be in Western libraries. These manuscripts were all derived from a common source, and no one of them contained chapters 1-5, & 7a. Since then two complete manuscripts of the texts have been discovered that are independent of each other and of the preceding group of texts, namely: the famous Codex Sinaiticus of the Bible (fourth century), in which the Epistle of Barnabas and "The Pastor" follow the books of the New Testament, and

---

[55] "The Ante-Nicene Fathers", Roberts & Donaldson, Vol 1, Buffalo: The Christian Literature Company 1885.

[56] However, it should be noted that the following Bible scholars have dated the epistle as follows. J. A. T. Robinson and J. B. Lightfoot dates it to the time of Emperor Vespasian (70-79 C.E.); P. Richardson and M. B. Shukster offer the time of Emperor Nero as the date of writing (96-98 C.E.); L. W. Barnard suggest the early part of Emperor Hadrian's reign (117-138 C.E.).

the Hierosolymitanus Codex, which includes the Didache.[57]

The epistle is found in the following authorities:

(1) The *Codex Sinaiticus*, an uncial of the fourth century, now at St. Petersburg, and published in photographic facsimile by the Clarendon Press.

(2) The 11th century Greek MS *Codex Hierosolymitanus*, found by Philotheos Byrennios[58] in 1873 in Constantinople, but now located in the library of the monastery of the Church of the Holy Sepulchre in Jerusalem.

(3) In eight defective MSS., in which owing to some accident the ninth chapter of the epistle of Polycarp is continued without a break by the fifth chapter of Barnabas. These MSS. are clearly descended from a common archetype, copied from a MS. in which Barnabas followed Polycarp, but the pages containing the end of the latter and beginning of the former were lost, and a copyist who did not observe this merged the one into the other.

(4) A Latin version, extant in a single MS. at St. Petersburg, in which the text stops at the end of chap. xvii. It thus omits the "Two Ways" teaching[59], and the question (perhaps insoluble) arises whether the Latin has omitted it, or the Greek interpolated it. At present the general opinion is in favour of the former view.

---

[57] Catholic Encyclopedia 1907

[58] A Greek Orthodox metropolitan of Nicomedia, Constantinople.

[59] For a description of the "two ways" teaching, see under chapter heading, "Teachings".

The epistle either is a general treatise, or was intended for some community in which Alexandrian ideas prevailed, though it is not possible to define either its destination, or the locality from which it was written with any greater accuracy. Its main object is to warn Christians against a Judaistic acceptance of the Old Testament, and the writer carries a symbolic exegesis as far as did Philo; indeed, he goes farther and apparently denies any literal significance at all to the commands of the Moral Law. The literal exegesis of the ceremonial law is to him a device of an evil angel who deceived the Jews.[60] He interpreted the Mosaic Law as if it were sheer allegory.

Writings

There are two apocryphal works connected with this Alexandrian Jew, the *Epistle of Barnabas* and the *Acts of Barnabas*, however, further research has revealed that the latter work was written post fourth century C.E. by another writer, and which will not be considered further herein. Although Clement of Alexandria thought, Barnabas of the NT had written the *Epistle of Barnabas*, Kollmann suggests this document was produced in the second century, after Barnabas had died (Kollmann, *Barnabas*, 54).[61]

Kitto's "Encyclopedia of Religious Knowledge" (article Barnabas) says of the writer of this epistle:

---

[60] Kirsopp Lake in *The Apostolic Fathers* (published London 1912), v. I, pp. 337-339.

[61] Tresham, A. K. (2012). Barnabas. In J. D. Barry & L. Wentz (Eds.), *The Lexham Bible Dictionary* (J. D. Barry & L. Wentz, Ed.). Bellingham, WA

He makes unauthorized additions to various parts of the Jewish Cultus; his views of the Old Economy are confused and erroneous; and he adopts a mode of interpretation countenanced by none of the inspired writers, and to the last degree puerile and absurd. The inference is unavoidable, that Barnabas, 'the son of prophecy,' 'the man full of the Holy Spirit and of faith,' was not the author of this epistle.

From a literary point of view, the Epistle of Barnabas has no merit. The style is tedious, poor in expression, deficient in clearness, elegance, and accuracy. The author's logic is weak, and his matter is not under his control; from this fact arise numerous digressions.[62] On perusing the epistle, the reader will be afforded an opportunity to judge this matter for himself. An extensive amount of the text of Barnabas is made up of quotations, largely from the LXX of Isaiah, but also from other canonical and non-canonical books.

> On perusing the Epistle, the reader will ... will consider the spirit and tone of the writing, as so decidedly opposed to all respect for Judaism—the numerous inaccuracies which it contains with respect to Mosaic enactments and observances—the absurd and trifling interpretations of Scripture which it suggests—and the many silly vaunts of superior knowledge in which its writer indulges.[63]

---

[62] Catholic Encyclopaedia 1907

[63] "Introductory Note to the Epistle of Barnabas", in The Ante-Nicene Fathers, Volume I: The Apostolic Fathers With Justin Martyr and

It is to be observed that this writer sometimes speaks as a Gentile, a fact which some have found it difficult to account for, on the supposition that he was a Hebrew, if not a Levite as well. But, so also did Paul sometimes speaks as a Roman, and sometimes as a Jew; and, owing to the mixed character of the early Church, he writes to the Romans (4:1) as if they were all Israelites, and again to the same Church (Rom. 11:13) as if they were all Gentiles. So this writer sometimes identifies himself with Jewish thought as a son of Abraham, and again speaks from the Christian position as if he were a Gentile, thus identifying himself with the catholicity of the Church.[64]

Teachings

The Epistle of Barnabas is significant because it is one of earliest attempts on the part of the Christian Community, outside of the New Testament, to reconcile itself with the Jewish Scriptures. This epistle is an exploration of the relationship between Christianity and Judaism at a time when the antagonism between the two is obviously still quite high. Its solution is to read everything in the Old Testament in the light of Jesus' life and teachings. Therefore, only the Christian understands the true meaning of the Scriptures [according to ch.10.12]. The sacrifice of Isaac, the goat that was led into the desert, Moses with his arms extended in the shape of the cross, and the serpent raised up in the desert are all figures, or "types" of Jesus Christ and his work of salvation. While all of these things are historically true,

Irenaeus, ed. Alexander Roberts, James Donaldson and A. Cleveland Coxe, 134 (Buffalo, NY: Christian Literature Company, 1885).

[64] "The Ante-Nicene Fathers", Roberts & Donaldson, Vol 1, Buffalo: The Christian Literature Company 1885.

the deeper significance is what they teach us about Jesus and how they pointed ahead to him. In addition, they are an affirmation of the pre-existence of Christ and his role in creation [5.5].

It appears that the motive behind the writing of the epistle was the author's fear that some Christian members were being swayed by teachings, which emphasize the lasting quality of the Jewish Covenant with God. Much of the document, therefore, is taken up with dismantling this idea and this so-called Barnabas does this by relating the story of the giving of the Law to Moses at Sinai (Exod. 24 ff). The point of this is to discover "whether he has given it [to the Jews]"(14.1). The author of the epistle then gives his own interpretation of the Sinai event. The Jews never received the Covenant because when Moses descended from Sinai he found them worshiping a golden calf. He threw down the tablets and, for the writer of Barnabas, the Covenant was forever broken (14.4). It is implied that the covenant then becomes hidden in Jesus and later given to the Gentiles through Jesus Christ. This is the reason he came to earth in the first place (14.5). There is no Christian precedent for making the claim that the Jewish people ever received the Covenant at Sinai. (It is in direct contradiction to the Biblical account in Exodus 34.10.) The author's radical stance on the Covenant may indicate that there were Christians who thought quite the opposite. It is likely that so-called Barnabas epistle was attempting to redress any claims that Jews still held a covenant with God, or even that there might be two Covenants - one for Jews and one for Gentiles. Barnabas draws a single line that does not allow for dual covenants. The teaching of the Two Ways[65] (18-21) reinforces this dichotomy but only in a general way.[66]

According to many scholars, the writer of the epistle teaches that it was never intended that the precepts of the Moral Law should be observed in their literal sense, that the Jews never had a covenant with God, and that circumcision was the work of the Devil, etc. Thus, he represents a unique point of view in the struggle against Judaism. It might be said more exactly that he condemned Jewish worship in its entirety because in his opinion, the Jews did not know how to rise to the spiritual and typical meaning, which God had in view when giving them the Law. It is this purely materialistic observance of the ceremonial ordinances, of which the literal fulfilment was insufficient, that the author holds to be the work of the Devil, and, according to him, the Jews never received the divine Covenant because they never understood its nature (ch. vii, 3, 11, ix, 7; x, 10; xiv).[67]

The epistle reinterprets many of the laws of the Torah in an allegorical[68] manner. For example, the prohibition on eating pork is not to be taken literally, but rather forbids the people to live like swine, who supposedly grunt when hungry but are silent when full:

---

[65] Regarding the "Two-Ways" teaching, see later under sub-heading, "Teachings".

[66] Ecole Initiative – an attempt to create a hypertext encyclopedia of early Christian church history on the Web.

[67] The Catholic Encyclopedia. New York: Robert Appleton Company. Retrieved May 11, 2013 from New Advent: http://www.newadvent.org/cathen/02299a.htm

[68] Allegory is an interpretive approach to Scripture that tries to find a hidden meaning when the literal meaning seems to provide little enlightenment.

likewise, the people are not to pray to God when they are in need but ignore him when they are satisfied. Similarly, the prohibition on eating rabbit means that the people are not to behave in a promiscuous manner, and the prohibition on eating weasel is actually to be interpreted as a prohibition of oral sex, based on the mistaken belief that weasels copulate via the mouth.[69]

From a Sabbath perspective, this epistle is important for two reasons: (1) It contains the first explicit references to the observance of Sunday as the "eighth day." (2) It reveals the social and political factors that contributed to the devaluation of the Sabbath and the adoption of Sunday worship by many early-century Christians. Consequently, Sunday worshippers to support their choice of worship day often quote the relevant portions of this epistle. In his attempt to defend the church from the influence of important Jewish institutions, Barnabas sets about emptying the Sabbath of all its validity for the present age. The great lengths to which he goes to repudiate the Sabbath expressly shows the continued influence the Sabbath had in Christianity at Alexandria during the time of his writing. This fact was somewhat problematical for those claiming that Christ and/or the Apostles issued direct commands to stop seventh-day Sabbath observance and start Sunday keeping. History shows clearly that most Christians kept the seventh-day Sabbath even as late as the fifth century C.E.[70]

---

[69] Ehrman, Bart D. (2005). *Lost Christianities: the battles for scripture and the faiths we never knew*. Oxford University Press. p. 146. ISBN 0-19-518249-9.

[70] Christian Publishing House is not in agreement with this writer. Christians are **not** under any obligation to keep a weekly Sabbath day. **(1)** The Sabbath observance was a sign between God and Israel (EX 31:16-17) **(2)** Christ was the end of the Law. (Rom 10:4; see also Gal

The final four chapters of the epistle spell out the writer's teaching concerning the "Two Ways", although the teaching does rate a mention in the earlier chapters (1-17). (We also find these at the beginning of the Didache, which may point to a common source for this teaching). There is the Way of Light and the Way of Darkness. The two ways are incompatible with each other and there can be no association between them. Light-giving angels guard one, the other by the angels of Satan. Those who follow the Way of Light will refrain from any sexual immorality, pride, lying, hatred or grudges. There is a specific prohibition against abortion and infanticide (19.5), and a strong admonition to discipline one's children. It also teaches respect for slaves and counsels those of the light to have a generous spirit. The Way of Darkness leads to eternal death and punishment because it is filled with all the things that destroy souls: "idolatry, audacity, exaltation of power, hypocrisy, duplicity, adultery, murder, robbery, arrogance, transgression, deceit, malice stubbornness, sorcery, magic art, greed, lack of fear of God" (20.1). The Epistle leaves no doubt that this is no dualistic battle

---

4:9-11; Eph. 2:13-16) **(3)** If you profaned the Sabbath, you were to be stoned to death. If the Sabbath is to be obeyed, this would still be in effect. (Col. 2:13-16; see also Ex 31:14 and Num. 15:32-35) **(4)** When the New Testament writers say the Mosaic Law was done away with, it is a reference also to the Ten Commandments, but not the principles. Many of the moral principles were restated in the New Testament. (Rom 7:6-7; 2 Cor. 3:7-11) **(5)** Doing away with the Mosaic Law, which includes the Ten Commandments, does not taking away of all moral restraint? (Heb. 8:10; Rom 6:15-17; Gal 5:18-21) **(6)** Actually on every seventh year, the Jews were to take the entire seventh year off from work. You do not hear the Christians who argue for the Sabbath, arguing this obligation. (Deut. 15:1, 2, 12; compare Deut. 14:28.)

between two equal powers. The Light always overcomes the darkness (John 1:5).[71]

Conclusion

The epistle contains numerous Scriptural errors and should therefore not be considered as inspired. It was never referred to by any of the New Testament writers (if written early [70-98 C.E.] like some have suggested), as Scripture, and it was not included in the New Testament canon by the majority of apostolic fathers.

Even though the Epistle of Barnabas is clearly not inspired, it does contain some interesting concepts. For instance, the author speaks out against abortion. It says in chapter 19, verse 5: "thou shalt not kill a child by abortion, neither shalt thou destroy it after it is born..."

The famous essay on "Snakes in Ireland" consisted of but three words, namely, "There are none." In like manner, so might we may dispose of the so-called "Epistle of Barnabas," for there is no such thing. In support of this statement, the following testimony is offered:

An epistle has come down to us bearing the name of Barnabas, but clearly not written by him ... The writer evidently was unacquainted with the Hebrew Scriptures, and has committed the blunder, among many others, of supposing that Abraham was familiar with the Greek alphabet some centuries before it existed.[72]

---

[71] 2011 American Bible Society, All Rights Reserved. 1865 Broadway, New York, NY 10023-7505

[72] McClintock and Strong's Encyclopaedia, art. Barnabas, Epistle of.

CHAPTER 5 Hermas - Early Christian Writer

Barry Hofstetter

Introduction

The Shepherd of Hermas is part of that collection of writings that since the 19th century has been termed "The Apostolic Fathers," the first generation of Christian leaders writing after the end of the apostolic age and the completion of the New Testament (NT) canonical documents. These writings are a vital part of our understanding regarding the development of Christianity. How did the ancient Christians understand the Gospel and apply it to their own context? We find in them a witness to the fact that certain documents of the NT were known to the ancient Christians. We see development regarding doctrine and practical issues which contribute significantly to the later history of the church. The Shepherd of Hermas is arguably somewhat later than some of the other documents in the collection (see below), but still provides a fascinating witness to the way in which one ancient author saw the *paradosis* (tradition) in application to his own context.[73] As we shall see, however, the author's conception of that tradition is quite different from the NT and even the other writings contemporaneous with him.

---

[73] I am using the Lightfoot edition of the Apostolic Fathers, both Greek (mostly) and English translation. The English translation is readily available on the Web, and though usually attributed to Lightfoot, was actually produced by his colleague J.R. Harmer, as the introductory note to the text indicates. Citations in this article are actually from the Logos collection, derived from the 1891 edition published by Macmillan and Co., London.

Summary, Structure and Genre

The Shepherd of Hermas begins with a Christian slave named Hermas who is sold by his master to a woman in Rome named Rhoda. He is apparently set free by her, and as a freedman goes on to live a moderately successful life engaging in the types of business to which freedmen were accustomed to pursue.[74] Many years later he sees her bathing in the Tiber river and is sorely tempted by her beauty. This moral lapse results in a great deal of soul searching on his behalf, and provides the segue into the rest of the work and its primary concern with the issues of what it means to live a moral Christian life, and particularly the issue of repentance. Hermas is the central character of the work with regard to whom these issues are explored. He successively meets, as he seeks to improve his life as a Christian, the Woman (the church) and the Shepherd (who may or may not stand in a position similar to that of the Lord). The work therefore take the shape of a novella or a morality play with a definite plot. It is divided historically into three sections, the Visions, the Mandates (precepts or instructions) and Similitudes (parables). Unlike a modern writing in which the author might endeavor to give each section more or less equal weight, these sections are not equal in either length or content. The Visions are actually introductory and provide what we might call now the "backstory" for the work. The great weight of the moral and theological instruction are contained in the second and third parts. The genre is partly in the form of an apocalypse, showing the triumph of the church over and

---

[74] Freedmen, *liberti*, were a very important part of the economic context of ancient Rome, providing the backbone of what today we would call the business and mercantile classes.

against the secular forces arrayed against her, and partly in the form of parables.

Authorship, Date and Provenance

There is more than one theory concerning the authorship of the work. One is that the Hermas of the story is the individual known to the apostle Paul (cf. Rom 16:14). This is by far the least likely theory, but demonstrates the tendency of both ancients and some moderns to make connections based on very tenuous facts, in this case the same name. Another theory is that Hermas was a contemporary of yet another of the apostolic fathers, Clement of Rome, and this connection is made from Vision 2.4.3:

> Thou shalt therefore write two little books, and shalt send one to Clement, and one to Grapte. So Clement shall send to the foreign cities, for this is his duty; while Grapte shall instruct the widows and the orphans. But thou shalt read (the book) to this city along with the elders that preside over the Church.[75]

This theory, based on actual textual evidence from the document, has much greater weight, but is still unlikely. The Clement mentioned is not referred to as presiding over the church at Rome, but seems to have the duty of passing correspondence on to "foreign" cities (Grk, "outside" cities), a duty which may or may not have belonged to someone of the rank of bishop, but one might expect a little more description if it was the bishop of Rome.

---

[75] Lightfoot, J. B., & Harmer, J. R. (1891). *The Apostolic Fathers* (409). London: Macmillan and Co.

The third and most likely theory is that Hermas was the brother of "Pope"[76] Pius the first of Rome (c. 140-155). The authority for this is the famous Muratorian Canon, a list of writings considered canonical or non-canonical by the compiler. This provides an external referent that in the absence of any competing facts to the contrary is likely to be accurate.

> But Hermas composed The Shepherd quite recently in our times in the city of Rome, while his brother, Pius, the bishop, occupied the [episcopal] seat of the city of Rome. [45] And therefore, it should indeed be read, but it cannot be published for the people in the Church, [46] neither among the Prophets, since their number is complete, [47] nor among the Apostles for it is after their time...[77]

Most scholars are agreed that the Muratorian Canon was originally composed in the second century, although some think it may have been as late as the fourth. It is on interesting grounds that the compiler rejects the canonicity of the text. We shall see below that that there are even more compelling reasons for not including it in the canon of Scripture.

If this is accurate, it also gives us the approximate date of the composition, which would be mid- to later second century A.D. This assumes single authorship of the text, something which several scholars dispute (for what I think are insufficient reasons, discussed below).

---

[76] The term "pope" of so early a figure is almost certainly anachronistic, but he is so called even by Protestant scholars.

[77] Found online at http://www.earlychristianwritings.com/text/muratorian-latin.html

The provenance is the place where the text was written. The simplest explanation would be city of Rome. The author in several places shows familiarity with the city and its environs, and clearly represents the action as taking place in that locale. Whether this is actually the case is less important than the fact that the church of Rome even in ancient times had a certain priority, both due to the legends of the apostles who had resided there and due its location in the capital of the empire. By placing the action there the writer lends a certain gravitas to the work which would help his readers take it more seriously.

Manuscripts and Language

An incomplete Greek copy of the Shepherd is included in codes Sinaiticus, perhaps the most important ancient manuscript left to us from ancient times. The other Greek manuscript (also incomplete) is the Athos manuscript, dating from the fourth century. There are also a number of Latin manuscripts in two distinct textual traditions (the Old Latin Version and the Palatine). These are complete. In the Lightfoot edition, the two Greek manuscripts are combined to produce the text, but the reader may be surprised that the final part of the text finishes in Latin. There is also an Aethiopic version, and occasional citations by ancient authorities, and especially Clement of Alexandria and Origen.[78]

The character of the Greek is quite interesting. The syntax (the actual grammar and order of the words) is quite simple. We have reasonably short sentences which tend to use a paratactic arrangement, similar to the style found in the Johannine writings in the NT. This means

---

[78] Lightfoot, p. 294-297.

that the author favors coordinating conjunctions rather than subordinate clauses or the equivalent, and avoids long sentences with several clauses. The style is very consistent throughout. This indicates to me that there is one author for the text, though arguably you could have an editor who simply made sure that the combined parts are consistent in style, but that seems less likely. Usually in a redacted text, one can find sufficient inconsistencies in style to at least make the case. If the reference to Clement is to the bishop of Rome, then this might indicate that the text was written in several parts over a long period of time, concluding in the mid-second century.

The author also seems to have a fairly limited vocabulary, which might indicate familiarity in Greek only with early Christian writings. Most of his vocabulary will be familiar to students of NT Greek. He tends to communicate the same ideas in the same words over and over again. This is often a feature of people who are writing in a second language that they do not know that well. A native or bi-lingual speaker of a language will often vary his vocabulary and expressions intuitively according to the context, but one who is not fluent but at a lesser level of mastery will tend to stay in the confines of what he has learned. If he is familiar with a particular body of literature or a particular linguaculture his speech and writing will reflect that. If in fact the provenance of the text is Rome, it may be that Hermas' first language was Latin, and that his Greek was limited to the Christian writings available to him and the Greek that may still have been spoken in the church of Rome at that time.

At the same time, like the NT authors, although his language would not be the polished and educated Greek of the literati, he still uses quite sophisticated literary devices and figures to communicate his content. This suggests to me that the style may actually be to some extent affected. In other words, he may be deliberately imitating the simpler style of the NT and other early Christians authors, for the simple reason that this might have sounded to his readers more authentic, much as Joseph Smith wrote the Book of Mormon in 17th century English, even though writing in the 19th century 200 hundred years after that dialect had gone out of style.

The Latin manuscripts faithfully represent the style of the Greek original.[79]

Comparison with the NT

Many years ago, I once had a dream, as a teenager and very young Christian, that I was visiting hell (along with several of my friends!). A demon came and gave us what looked like a NT. As I opened it up and read it, with a sinking feeling I realized it was nothing like the Bible that I had already come to cherish. This is precisely how many Christians feel when they read the Shepherd of Hermas. It clearly borrows imagery and ideas from canonical materials and the early Christian tradition, yet in content it is significantly different from the majority of the NT.

Specifically it maintains what many would call salvation by works and a very strict code of moralism as the rule for the Christian life. This can be seen by a simple vocabulary study (in addition to reading the actual content). The word grace (Grk., *charis*) appears four times in the Shepherd, and in the more general sense of "gift" or "favor," and not the semi-technical sense of

---

[79] I can't comment on the Aethiopic, since I know nothing about that language.

"divine forgiveness" that it often has in the NT. In contrast, in the NT, the same word appears 155 times, the majority of these in the Pauline epistles. Grace is clearly not an important concept for the author of the Shepherd. By contrast, repentance (Grk., *metanoia*) appears 13 times in the Shepherd and the verb repent (Grk., *metanoeo*) appears 93 times. The verb appears 34 times in the NT and the noun 22 times. While word studies are not the whole story (the context and usage of the words is very important) here it reveals a clear difference in the emphasis, indeed, a difference in conceptualization, between the Shepherd and the NT. For Hermas, the focus is on the deeds of the individual, and particularly repentance, and not on the work of grace from God that produces that repentance, as in in the NT.

This becomes even clearer when we read the actual content of the Shepherd. One of the major problems of the early church was repentance after baptism. Baptism covered sin up until the time of the baptism, but what if one sinned after baptism? Related to his was the problem of lapsing during persecution. If one recanted the faith in order to save his life and property, could he then repent and return to the fold after the persecution was over? You can imagine the very human reaction of many who remained faithful and suffered great loss. Their answer was often a resounding "no!" and this led directly to the "second repentence" controversy. Because of The Shepherd's handling of this, some have dated the text later, but it was an issue of continuing concern for the ancient church, and was applicable to all sins, not just lapsing under persecution. The Shepherd's answer to this issue is that one repentance for sin after baptism is acceptable, but no more.

After that thou hast made known unto them all these words, which the Master commanded me that they should be revealed unto thee, then all their sins which they sinned aforetime are forgiven to them; yea, and to all the saints that have sinned unto this day, if they repent with their whole heart, and remove double-mindedness from their heart. 5For the Master sware by His own glory, as concerning His elect; that if, now that this day has been set as a limit, sin shall hereafter be committed, they shall not find salvation; for repentance for the righteous hath an end; the days of repentance are accomplished for all the saints; whereas for the Gentiles there is repentance until the last day.[80]

Sir,' say I, 'to ask a further question.' 'Speak on,' saith he. 'I have heard, Sir,' say I, 'from certain teachers, that there is no other repentance, save that which took place when we went down into the water and obtained remission of our former sins.'...But I say unto you,' saith he, 'if after this great and holy calling any one, being tempted of the devil, shall commit sin, he hath only one (opportunity of) repentance.[81]

Now, what would the NT perspective on this be? Is there a limit on forgiveness for sins? For one thing, baptism is seen as a sign and symbol for the forgiveness

---

[80] Lightfoot, J. B., & Harmer, J. R. (1891). *The Apostolic Fathers* (408). London: Macmillan and Co.

[81] Lightfoot, J. B., & Harmer, J. R. (1891). *The Apostolic Fathers* (425). London: Macmillan and Co.

of sins, not that which actually produces that forgiveness. In the NT, it is particularly faith which obtains forgiveness. Of the many verses that could be cited:

> [21] But now the righteousness of God has been manifested apart from the law, although the Law and the Prophets bear witness to it— [22] the righteousness of God through faith in Jesus Christ for all who believe. For there is no distinction: [23] for all have sinned and fall short of the glory of God, [24] and are justified by his grace as a gift, through the redemption that is in Christ Jesus, [25] whom God put forward as a propitiation by his blood, to be received by faith. This was to show God's righteousness, because in his divine forbearance he had passed over former sins. [26] It was to show his righteousness at the present time, so that he might be just and the justifier of the one who has faith in Jesus. [82]

We also have:

> If we confess our sins, he is faithful and just to forgive us our sins and to cleanse us from all unrighteousness. [83]

> My little children, I am writing these things to you so that you may not sin. But if anyone

---

[82] The Holy Bible: English Standard Version. 2001 (Ro 3:21–26). Wheaton: Standard Bible Society.

[83] The Holy Bible: English Standard Version. 2001 (1 Jn 1:9). Wheaton: Standard Bible Society.

does sin, we have an advocate with the Father, Jesus Christ the righteous.[84]

From these and other NT passages, a case could be made that there is no limit at all to forgiveness of sins. One issue that the Shepherd is clearly concerned with is antinomianism, the idea that one can, after having received forgiveness, sin with impunity. The answer the Shepherd invents is that this simply means one loses his salvation. Even if one repentance is valid after baptism, that is still essentially salvation by works. The answer of the NT is that forgiveness is radical, total and eternal, but if that forgiveness is truly obtained, then it results in a completely different lifestyle for the individual. The Christian will become concerned with living in gratitude to God for the immense gift he has received. When he does sin, he will grieve, and immediately seek to restore his relationship with God. It is the love of God which is the motivation for living a moral life in the NT. It is the fear of God, not in the biblical sense of awe or reverence, but in the sense of true fear, of losing eternal life and eternal punishment, that is presented as the motivation in the Shepherd.

Conclusion

The Shepherd is an important document from early church history, a witness to the different ways in which the early Christian tradition could be interpreted. From a literary perspective it is a fascinating use of allegory and parable used to communicate its message. From a biblical and evangelical perspective however, the doctrine of the work is completely contrary to the Gospel. For this reason the ancient church did well not to include it in the

---

[84] *The Holy Bible: English Standard Version*. 2001 (1 Jn 2:1). Wheaton: Standard Bible Society.

canon, and not simply because it was a later work not to be included with the apostles. It reminds us that heresy can be produced at any time, and even become popular in certain circles, and that we must be ever vigilant to guard the truth as expressed in the canonical Scriptures. Reading the Shepherd and other writings produced after the completion of the NT also highlights the superiority of the NT with its high view of soteriology (salvation) and Christology (doctrine of Christ), both of which are severely lacking in the Shepherd.

CHAPTER 6 Papias - Enjoyed the Lord's Sayings

Papias (writing in the first third of the 2nd century)[85] was a bishop of the early Church. Eusebius of Caesarea calls him "Bishop of Hierapolis" (modern Pamukkale, Turkey), which is 22 km from Laodicea and near Colossae (see Col. 4:12-13), in the Lycus river valley in Phrygia, Asia Minor, not to be confused with the Hierapolis of Syria.

He wrote extensively about the Christian Oral Tradition. The Interpretations of the Sayings of the Lord (his word for "sayings" is logia) in five books, would have been a prime early authority in the exegesis of the sayings of Jesus, some of which are recorded in the Gospel of Matthew and the Gospel of Luke, however the book has not survived and is known only through fragments quoted in later writers, with approval in Irenaeus's Against Heresies and later by Eusebius in Ecclesiastical History, the earliest surviving history of the early Church.

Papias describes his way of gathering information:

---

[85] http://en.wikipedia.org/wiki/Papias_of_Hierapolis

63

I will not hesitate to add also for you to my interpretations what I formerly learned with care from the Presbyters and have carefully stored in memory, giving assurance of its truth. For I did not take pleasure as the many do in those who speak much, but in those who teach what is true, nor in those who relate foreign precepts, but in those who relate the precepts which were given by the Lord to the faith and came down from the Truth itself. And also if any follower of the Presbyters happened to come, I would inquire for the sayings of the Presbyters, what Andrew said, or what Peter said, or what Philip or what Thomas or James or what John or Matthew or any other of the Lord's disciples, and for the things which other of the Lord's disciples, and for the things which Aristion and the Presbyter John, the disciples of the Lord, were saying. For I considered that I should not get so much advantage from matter in books as from the voice which yet lives and remains.[86]

Thus Papias reports he heard things that came from an unwritten, oral tradition of the Presbyters, a "sayings" or logia tradition that had been passed from Jesus to such of the apostles and disciples as he mentions in the fragmentary quote. The scholar Helmut Koester considers him the earliest surviving witness of this tradition.[87]

Eusebius held Papias in low esteem, perhaps because of his work's influence in perpetuating, through Irenaeus

---

[86] Michael William Holmes, The Apostolic Fathers in English, page 309 (Baker Academic, 2006).

[87] Ancient Christian Gospels (Harrisburg: Trinity Press, 1990), pp. 32f

and others, belief in a millennial reign of Christ upon earth, that would soon usher in a new Golden Age. Eusebius calls Papias 'a man of small mental capacity[88] who mistook the figurative language of apostolic traditions'. Whether this was so to any degree is difficult to judge without the text available. However, Papias's millennialism (according to Anastasius of Sinai, along with Clement of Alexandria and Ammonius he understood the Six Days (Hexaemeron) and the account of Paradise as referring mystically to Christ and His Church) was nearer in spirit to the actual Christianity of the sub-apostolic age, especially in western Anatolia (e.g., Montanism), than Eusebius realized.[89]

Traditions related by Papias

About the origins of the Gospels, Papias (as quoted by Eusebius) Quoting John the Elder wrote:

`And this the Presbyter used to say [this is in the plural implying John the Elder would employ this argument multiple times in defense of Mark's Gospel]: "Mark, being the recorder of Peter, wrote accurately but not in order whatever he [Peter] remembered of the things either said or done by the Lord; for he [Mark] had neither heard the Lord nor followed him, but later, as I said, Peter, who used to make teachings according to the cheias, [a special kind of anecdote] but not making as it were a

---

[88] Historia Ecclesiastica 3.39.13.

[89] See Funk, fragments 6 and 7; translated by Michael W. Holmes in The Apostolic Fathers in English (Grand Rapids: Baker Academic, 2006), p. 314.

systematic composition of the Lord's sayings; so that Mark did not err at all when he wrote certain things just as he had recalled [them]. For he had but one intention, not to leave out anything he had heard, nor to falsify anything in them". This is what was related by Papias about Mark. But about Matthew`s this was said: "For Matthew composed the logia [sayings] in Hebrew style; but each recorded them as he was able"`[90] [author incomplete]. This last part is translated into English as everyone interpreted them as he was able by Dr. Arthur C. McGiffert and Dr. Ernest C. Richardson.[91]

Citing this text, many argue that Papias claimed that Matthew was written in the Hebrew language, (as it is often translated in English). This claim of the Semitic origins (Aramaic primacy or Hebrew primacy) of the New testament writings is also testified to by other Church Fathers including Ireneus, Origen, Eusebius, Pantaeneus, Epiphanius, Jerome, Isho'dad, as well as, Clement of Alexandria. Some would argue, however, that Papias' comment in Greek, "Hebrew dialect" is a common construction in Greek and is seen in many different sources and contexts and seems to consistently refer to a style or subset of a language being spoken; and, this is distinguished from the general Greek term for language or tongue. Papias' statement seems to signify a style of language or dialect being used by the "Hebrews",

---

[90] Eusebius, Church History, Book 3, Chapter 39.15-16

[91] Eusebius, Church History, Book 3, Chapter 39.16, translated by Dr. Arthur C. McGiffert and Dr. Ernest C. Richardson, Nicene and Post-Nicene Library of the Christian Fathers, WM. B. EERDMANS PUBLISHING COMPANY, GRAND RAPIDS, MICHIGAN, 1890

(or in other words, the style or subset of a language being used by the Hebrew race). In the historical context, the "dialect of the Hebrews", was most probably a reference to the Hebrew dialect of Aramaic. Due to the testimony of so many other sources, including Papias' contemporaries, this argument seem likely to overlook the other sources for this same claim. In fact all of the previously listed Church Fathers are quoted in their own writings as testifying to the Semitic origins of, at the very least, the Gospel of Matthew. Other scholars on the language of the New Testament have also argued that at least portions of the New Testament writings were originally penned in a Semitic tongue.

There is question whether the documents which Papias knew as the Gospels of Matthew and Mark are the same ones that we have today: Matthew is a narrative, rather than a sayings gospel with commentary, and some scholars reject the thesis that it was originally written in Hebrew. (See the Gospel according to the Hebrews.)[92]

Papias also related a number of traditions that Eusebius had characterized as "some strange parables and teachings of the savior, and some other more mythical accounts."[93] For example, Eusebius indicated that Papias heard stories about Justus, surnamed Barsabas, who drank poison but suffered no harm and another story via

---

[92] For a more detailed discussion of this passage, see Raymond E. Brown, An Introduction to the New Testament (New York: Doubleday, 1997), pp. 158ff, on which the material in this paragraph is based.

[93] However, G.A. Williamson's translation for Penguin Classics (New York, 1965, pp. 151f) puts this passage in these words: "some otherwise unknown parables and teachings of the Saviour, and other things of a more allegorical character." / It remains unknown whether or not these were earlier versions of the Jesus story. Papias only informs his reader of their existence, nothing else.

a daughter of Philip the Evangelist concerning the resurrection of a corpse.[94]

Eusebius states that Papias "reproduces a story about a woman falsely accused before the Lord of many sins." J. B. Lightfoot identified this story with the Pericope Adulterae, and included it in his collection of fragments of Papias' work. However, Michael W. Holmes has pointed out that it is not certain "that Papias knew the story in precisely this form, inasmuch as it now appears that at least two independent stories about Jesus and a sinful woman circulated among Christians in the first two centuries of the church, so that the traditional form found in many New Testament manuscripts may well represent a conflation of two independent shorter, earlier versions of the incident."[95]

According to a scholium attributed to Apollinaris of Laodicea, Papias also related a tradition on the death of Judas Iscariot:

> Judas did not die by hanging, but lived on, having been cut down before he was suffocated. And the Acts of the Apostles show this, that falling head long he burst asunder in the midst, and all his bowels gushed out. This fact is related more clearly by Papias, the disciple of John, and the fourth book of the Expositions of the Oracles of the Lord as follows:

---

[94] Hist. Eccl. 3.39.

[95] Holmes, The Apostolic Fathers, p. 304. This observation was first made by Bart D. Ehrman, "Jesus and the Adulteress," New Testament Studies 34 (1988) 24-44.

Judas walked about in this world a terrible example of impiety; his flesh swollen to such an extent that, where hay wagon can pass with ease, he was not able to pass, no, not even the mass of his head merely. They say that his eyelids swelled to such an extent that he could not see the light at all, while as for his eyes they were not visible even by a physician looking through an instrument, so far have they sunk from the surface.

His genitals appeared entirely disfigured, nauseous and large. When he carried himself about discharge and worms flowed from his entire body through his private areas only, on account of his outrages. After many agonies and punishments, he died in his own place. And on account of this the place is desolate and uninhabited even now. And to this day no one is able to go by that place, except if they block their noses with their hands. Such judgment was spread through his body and upon the earth.[96]

Papias' Dates

Concerning the date of his writing, there is Irenaeus' statement, later in the 2nd century, that Papias was "a hearer of John, and companion of Polycarp, a man of old time." (Adversus Haereses V 33.4) If Polycarp was in fact born not later than AD 69, then there may be no reason to depend on a further, but disputed tradition, that Papias shared in the martyrdom of Polycarp (ca AD

---

[96] A catena compiled by Cramer vol 3 p12 (translation from chronicon.net)

155). In sum, the fact that Irenaeus thought of Papias as Polycarp's contemporary and "a man of the old time," together with the affinity between the religious tendencies described in the fragment from Papias's Preface quoted by Eusebius and those reflected in the Epistles of Ignatius and of Polycarp, all point to his having flourished in the first quarter of the 2nd century.

Indeed, Eusebius, who deals with him along with Clement and Ignatius (rather than Polycarp) under the reign of Trajan, and before referring at all to Hadrian's reign, suggests that he wrote "as early as 110 and probably no later than the early 130s, with several scholars opting for the earlier end of the spectrum".[97] No known fact is inconsistent with c. 60-135 as the period of Papias's life. It should be noted that, though he was probably writing as an old man in Hierapolis, the enquiries he made took place a long time beforehand, and some of his eyewitnesses could well have met Jesus or the Apostles, or both. Eusebius (3.36) calls him "bishop" of Hierapolis, but whether with good ground is uncertain. In this putative capacity as bishop, Papias was supposedly succeeded by Abercius of Hieropolis.

---

[97] C.E. Hill (2006), p.309

CHAPTER 7 Justin Martyr - Early Apologist

Justin Martyr, also known as Saint Justin (100–ca.165 C.E.),[98] was an early Christian apologist, and is regarded as the foremost interpreter of the theory of the Logos in the 2nd century.[99] Most of his works are lost, but two apologies and a dialogue did survive. He is considered a saint by the Roman Catholic Church, the Anglican Church, and the Eastern Orthodox Church.

Early Life and Ministry

Most of what is known about the life of Justin Martyr comes from his own writings. He was born at Flavia Neapolis (today Nablus) in Palestine into a pagan family, and defined himself as a Gentile.[100] His grandfather, Bacchius, had a Greek name, while his father, Priscus, bore a Latin name, which has led to speculations that his ancestors may have settled in Neapolis soon after its establishment or that they were descended from a Roman 'diplomatic' community that had been sent there.[101] He received a Greek education. He tells us (Dialogue 2-8) that he tried first the school of

---

[98] http://en.wikipedia.org/wiki/Justin_Martyr

[99] Rokeah (2002) Justin Martyr and the Jews p.22.

[100] Craig D. Allert, Revelation, Truth, Canon, and Interpretation: Studies in Just in Martyr's Dialogue With Trypho, page 28 (Leiden, Brill, 2002).

[101] Reinhold Plummer,Early Christian authors on Samaritans and Samaritanism, Mohr Siebeck, 2002 p.14.

a Stoic philosopher, who was unable to explain God's being to him. He then attended a Peripatetic philosopher but was put off because the philosopher was too eager for his fee. Then he went to hear a Pythagorean philosopher who demanded that he first learn music, astronomy and geometry, which he did not wish to do. Subsequently, he adopted Platonism after encountering a Platonist thinker who had recently settled in his city. Some time afterwards, he chanced upon an old man, possibly a Palestinian or Syrian Christian,[102] in the vicinity of the seashore, who engaged him in a dialogue about God and spoke of the testimony of the prophets as being more reliable than the reasoning of philosophers. It was this argument, Justin avers, which kindled in him a love of Christ and led him to embrace Christianity.[103] He was influenced in this decision by the fearless conduct of Christians who were facing execution (Apol. 2:12). His conversion is commonly assumed to have taken place at Ephesus[104] though it may have occurred anywhere on the road from Palestine to Rome.[105]

He then adopted the dress of a philosopher himself and traveled about teaching. During the reign of Antoninus Pius (138-161), he arrived in Rome and started his own school. Tatian was one of his pupils.[106] In the

---

[102] Oskar Skarsaune, The proof from prophecy: a study in Justin Martyr's proof-text tradition:text-type, provenance, theological profile, Brill, 1987 p.246.

[103] Dialogue with Trypho, chapters 3-8.

[104] J. Quasten, Patrology vol. 1, p.196-7. / Plummer, 2002 p.15.

[105] Skarsaune, The proof from prophecy,pp.245-6 and notes 1 and 2.

[106] Marian Hillar, From Logos to Trinity: The Evolution of Religious Beliefs from Pythagoras to Tertullian, page 139 (Cambridge University Press, 2012).

reign of Marcus Aurelius, after disputing with the cynic philosopher Crescens, he was denounced by the latter to the authorities, according to Tatian (Address to the Greeks 19) and Eusebius (HE IV 16.7-8). Justin was tried, together with six companions, by Junius Rusticus, who was urban prefect from 163-167, and was beheaded, probably in 165. The martyrdom of Justin preserves the court record of the trial.[107]

The church of St. John the Baptist in Sacrofano, a few miles north of Rome, claims to have his relics.[108]

In 1882 Pope Leo XIII had a Mass and an Office composed for his feast day, which he set at 14 April,[109] one day after the date of his death as indicated in the Martyrology of Florus; but since this date quite often falls within the main Paschal celebrations, the feast was moved in 1968 to 1 June, the date on which he has been celebrated in the Byzantine Rite since at least the 9th century.[110]

Writings

The earliest mention of Justin is found in the Oratio ad Graecos by Tatian who, after calling him "the most admirable Justin," quotes a saying of his and says that the Cynic Crescens laid snares for him. Irenaeus[111] speaks of

---

[107] J. Quasten, Patrology vol. 1, p.196-7.

[108] Sacrofano - Church of Saint John the Baptist, "...the bones of St. Justin are preserved in a great urn under the coloured marble high altar, built in 1515."

[109] Catholic Encyclopedia: St. Justin Martyr

[110] Calendarium Romanum (Libreria Editrice Vaticana 1969), p. 94

[111] Haer. I., xxviii. 1.

Justin's martyrdom and of Tatian as his disciple. Irenaeus quotes Justin twice[112] and shows his influence in other places. Tertullian, in his Adversus Valentinianos, calls Justin a philosopher and a martyr and the earliest antagonist of heretics. Hippolytus and Methodius of Olympus also mention or quote him. Eusebius of Caesarea deals with him at some length,[113] and names the following works:

(1) The First Apology addressed to Antoninus Pius, his sons, and the Roman Senate;[114]

(2) a Second Apology addressed to the Roman Senate;

(3) the Discourse to the Greeks, a discussion with Greek philosophers on the character of their gods;

(4) an Hortatory Address to the Greeks;

(5) a treatise On the Sovereignty of God, in which he makes use of pagan authorities as well as Christian;

(6) a work entitled The Psalmist;

(7) a treatise in scholastic form On the Soul; and

(8) the Dialogue with Trypho.

Eusebius implies that other works were in circulation; from St Irenaeus he knows of the apology "Against Marcion," and from Justin's "Apology"[115] of a

---

[112] IV., vi. 2, V., xxvi. 2.

[113] Church History, iv. 18.

[114] David Rokéah, Justin Martyr and the Jews, page 2 (Leiden, Brill, 2002).

[115] i. 26

"Refutation of all Heresies".[116] Epiphanius[117] and St Jerome[118] mention Justin.

Rufinus borrows from his Latin original of Hadrian's letter.

After Rufinus, Justin was known mainly from St Irenaeus and Eusebius or from spurious works. The Chronicon Paschale assigns his martyrdom to the year 165. A considerable number of other works are given as Justin's by Arethas, Photius, and other writers, but this attribution is now generally admitted to be spurious. The Expositio rectae fidei has been assigned by Draseke to Apollinaris of Laodicea, but it is probably a work of as late as the 6th century. The Cohortatio ad Graecos has been attributed to Apollinaris of Laodicea, Apollinaris of Hierapolis, as well as others. The Epistola ad Zenam et Serenum, an exhortation to Christian living, is dependent upon Clement of Alexandria, and is assigned by Pierre Batiffol to the Novatian Bishop Sisinnius (c. 400). The extant work under the title "On the Sovereignty of God" does not correspond with Eusebius' description of it, though Harnack regards it as still possibly Justin's, and at least of the 2nd century. The author of the smaller treatise To the Greeks cannot be Justin, because he is dependent on Tatian; Harnack places it between 180 and 240.

Apology

---

[116] Church History, IV., xi. 10.

[117] Haer., xlvi. 1.

[118] De vir. ill., ix.

The Dialogue is a later work than the First Apology; the date of composition of the latter, judging from the fact that it was addressed to Antoninus Pius and his adopted sons Marcus Aurelius and Lucius Verus, must fall between 147 and 161.

Dialogue with Trypho

In the Dialogue with Trypho, after an introductory section, Justin undertakes to show that Christianity is the new law for all men.

On The Resurrection

The fragments of the work "On the Resurrection" begin with the assertion that the truth, and God the author of truth, need no witness, but that as a concession to the weakness of men it is necessary to give arguments to convince those who gainsay it. It is then shown, after a denial of unfounded deductions, that the resurrection of the body is neither impossible nor unworthy of God, and that the evidence of prophecy is not lacking for it. Another fragment takes up the positive proof of the resurrection, adducing that of Christ and of those whom he recalled to life. In yet another fragment the resurrection is shown to be that of what has gone down, i.e., the body; the knowledge concerning it is the new doctrine, in contrast to that of the old philosophers. The doctrine follows from the command to keep the body in moral purity.

The treatise On the Resurrection, of which extensive fragments are preserved in the Sacra parallela, is not so generally accepted. Even earlier than this collection, it is referred to by Procopius of Gaza (c. 465-528). Methodius appeals to Justin in support of his interpretation of 1 Corinthians 15:50 in a way which makes it natural to assume the existence of a treatise on the subject, to say nothing of other traces of a connection in thought both here in Irenaeus (V., ii.-xiii. 5) and in Tertullian, where it is too close to be anything but a conscious following of the Greek. The Against Marcion is lost, as is the Refutation of all Heresies to which Justin himself refers in Apology, i. 26; Hegesippus, besides perhaps Irenaeus and Tertullian, seems to have used it.

Role within the Church

Flacius discovered "blemishes" in Justin's theology, which he attributed to the influence of pagan philosophers; and in modern times Semler and S.G. Lange have made him out a thorough Hellene, while Semisch and Otto defend him from this charge.

In opposition to the school of Ferdinand Christian Baur, who considered him a Jewish Christian, Albrecht Ritschl has pointed out that it was precisely because he was a Gentile Christian that he did not fully understand the Old Testament foundation of Paul's teaching, and explained in this way the modified character of his Paulinism and his legal mode of thought.

M. von Engelhardt has attempted to extend this line of treatment to Justin's entire theology, and to show that his conceptions of God, of free will and righteousness, of redemption, grace, and merit prove the influence of the cultivated Greek pagan world of the 2nd century, dominated by the Platonic and Stoic philosophy.

But he admits that Justin is a Christian in his unquestioning adherence to the Church and its faith, his unqualified recognition of the Old Testament, and his faith in Christ as the Son of God the Creator, made manifest in the flesh, crucified, and risen, through which belief he succeeds in getting away from the dualism of both pagan and Gnostic philosophy.

Justin was confident that his teaching was that of the Church at large. He knows of a division among the orthodox only on the question of the millennium and on the attitude toward the milder Jewish Christianity, which he personally is willing to tolerate as long as its professors in their turn do not interfere with the liberty of the Gentile converts; his millenarianism seems to have no connection with Judaism, but he believes firmly in a millennium, and generally in the Christian eschatology.

Justin saw himself as a scholar, although his skills in Hebrew were either non-existent or minimal. His opposition to Judaism was typical of church leaders in his day but does not descend to the level of anti-semitism. After collaborating with a Jewish convert to assist him with Hebrew, Justin published an attack on Judaism based upon a no-longer-extant text of a Midrash. This Midrash was reconstructed and published by Saul Lieberman.

Conversion and teachings

Justin had, like others, the idea that the Greek philosophers had derived, if not borrowed, the most essential elements of truth found in their teaching from the Old Testament. But at the same time he adopted the Stoic doctrine of the "seminal word," and so philosophy was to him an operation of the Word—in fact, through his identification of the Word with Christ, it was brought into immediate connection with him.[119]

Thus he does not scruple to declare that Socrates and Heraclitus were Christians (Apol., i. 46, ii. 10). His aim, of course, is to emphasize the absolute significance of Christ, so that all that ever existed of virtue and truth may be referred to him. The old philosophers and law-givers had only a part of the Logos, while the whole appears in Christ.[120]

While the gentile peoples, seduced by demons, had deserted the true God for idols, the Jews and Samaritans possessed the revelation given through the prophets and awaited the Messiah. The law, however, while containing commandments intended to promote the true fear of God, had other prescriptions of a purely pedagogic nature, which necessarily ceased when Christ, their end, appeared; of such temporary and merely relative regulations were circumcision, animal sacrifices, the Sabbath, and the laws as to food. Through Christ the abiding law of God has been fully proclaimed. In his character as the teacher of the new doctrine and promulgator of the new law lies the essential nature of his redeeming work.[121]

The idea of an economy of grace, of a restoration of the union with God which had been destroyed by sin, is not foreign to him. It is noteworthy that in the

---

[119] New Schaff-Herzog Encyclopedia of Religious Knowledge 3rd ed. 1914.

[120] New Schaff-Herzog Encyclopedia of Religious Knowledge 3rd ed. 1914.

[121] New Schaff-Herzog Encyclopedia of Religious Knowledge 3rd ed. 1914.

"Dialogue" he no longer speaks of a "seed of the Word" in every man, and in his non-apologetic works the emphasis is laid upon the redeeming acts of the life of Christ rather than upon the demonstration of the reasonableness and moral value of Christianity, though the fragmentary character of the latter works makes it difficult to determine exactly to what extent this is true and how far the teaching of Irenaeus on redemption is derived from him.[122]

Doctrine of the logos

Justin's use of the idea of the Logos has always attracted attention. It is probably too much to assume a direct connection with Philo of Alexandria in this particular. The idea of the Logos was widely familiar to educated men, and the designation of the Son of God as the Logos was not new to Christian theology. The significance is clear, however, of the manner in which Justin identifies the historical Christ with the rational force operative in the universe, which leads up to the claim of all truth and virtue for the Christians and to the demonstration of the adoration of Christ, which aroused so much opposition, as the only reasonable attitude. It is mainly for this justification of the worship of Christ that Justin employs the Logos-idea, though where he explicitly deals with the divinity of the Redeemer and his relation to the Father, he makes use of the Old Testament, not of the Logos-idea, which thus cannot be said to form an essential part of his Christology.[123]

---

[122] New Schaff-Herzog Encyclopedia of Religious Knowledge 3rd ed. 1914.

[123] New Schaff-Herzog Encyclopedia of Religious Knowledge 3rd ed. 1914.

The 1913 Catholic Encyclopedia notes that scholars have differed on whether Justin's writings on the nature of God were meant to express his firm opinion on points of doctrine, or to speculate on these matters. Specific points Justin addressed include that the Logos is "numerically distinct from the Father" though "born of the very substance of the Father", and that through the "through the Word, God has made everything". Justin used a metaphor of fire, to describe the Logos as spreading like a flame, rather than "dividing" the substance of the father. He also defended the Holy Spirit as a member of the Trinity, as well as the birth of Jesus to his mother Mary when she was a virgin. The Encyclopedia states that Justin places the genesis of the Logos as a voluntary act of the Father at the beginning of creation, noting that this is an "unfortunate" conflict with later Christian teachings.[124]

---

[124] 1913 Old Catholic Encyclopedia, "St. Justin Martyr"

The Word is numerically distinct from the Father (Dial., cxxviii, cxxix; cf. lvi, lxii). He was born of the very substance of the Father, not that this substance was divided, but He proceeds from it as one fire does from another at which it is lit (cxxviii, lxi); this form of production (procession) is compared also with that of human speech (lxi). The Word (Logos) is therefore the Son: much more, He alone may properly be called Son (II Apol., vi, 3); He is the monogenes, the unigenitus (Dial., cv). Elsewhere, however, Justin, like St. Paul, calls Him the eldest Son, prototokos (I Apol., xxxiii; xlvi; lxiii; Dial., lxxxiv, lxxxv, cxxv). The Word is God (I Apol., lxiii; Dial., xxxiv, xxxvi, xxxvii, lvi, lxiii, lxxvi, lxxxvi, lxxxvii, cxiii, cxv, cxxv, cxxvi, cxviii). His Divinity, however, seems subordinate, as does the worship which is rendered to Him (I Apol., vi; cf. lxi, 13; Teder, "Justins des Märtyrers Lehre von Jesus Christus", Freiburg im Br., 1906, 103-19). The Father engendered Him by a free and voluntary act (Dial., lxi, c, cxxvii, cxxviii; cf. Teder, op. cit., 104), at the beginning of all His works (Dial., lxi, lxii, II Apol., vi, 3); in this last text certain authors thought they distinguished in the Word two states of being, one intimate, the other outspoken, but this distinction, though found in some other apologists, is in Justin very doubtful. Through the Word God has made everything (II Apol., vi;

81

Memoirs of the apostles

Justin Martyr, in his First Apology (ca. 155) and Dialogue with Trypho (ca. 160),[125] sometimes refers to written sources consisting of narratives of the life of Jesus and quotations of the sayings of Jesus as "memoirs of the apostles" (Greek transliteration: apomnêmoneúmata tôn apostólôn) and less frequently as gospels (Greek transliteration: euangélion) which, Justin says, were read every Sunday in the church at Rome (1 Apol. 67.3 – "and the memoirs of the apostles or the writings of the prophets are being read as long as it is allowable").[126]

The designation "memoirs of the apostles" occurs twice in Justin's First Apology (66.3, 67.3–4) and thirteen

---

Dial., cxiv). The Word is diffused through all humanity (I Apol., vi; II, viii; xiii); it was He who appeared to the patriarchs (I Apol., lxii; lxiii; Dial., lvi, lix, lx etc.). Two influences are plainly discernible in the aforesaid body of doctrine. It is, of course, to Christian revelation that Justin owes his concept of the distinct personality of the Word, His Divinity and Incarnation; but philosophic speculation is responsible for his unfortunate concepts of the temporal and voluntary generation of the Word, and for the subordinationism of Justin's theology. It must be recognized, moreover, that the latter ideas stand out more boldly in the "Apology" than in the "Dialogue."

[125] Rokeah (2002) Justin Martyr and the Jews p. 2 – His First Apology dates from about 155 CE, for it mentions (chap. 29) the procurator of Egypt, Felix, who served in this capacity between 151 and 154. Grant (Greek Apologists pp. 53–54) links the First Apology to the martyrdom of Polycarp, the bishop of Smyrna, which occurred in 155 or 156; he finds allusions in the Apology to the description of Polycarp's death at the stake found in a letter sent by the Christian community of Smyrna to other Christian communities immediately after the event. ... The First Apology is mentioned in the Dialogue (end of chap. 120), and it is therefore likely that the latter was composed around 160 CE."

[126] Koester (1990) Ancient Christian Gospels p. 38 – "It is clear that these "memoirs" are indeed gospel writings and that they are used liturgically as instructions for the sacrament and as texts for homilies."

times in the Dialogue, mostly in his interpretation of Psalm 22, whereas the term "gospel" is used only three times, once in 1 Apol. 66.3 and twice in the Dialogue. The single passage where Justin uses both terms (1 Apol. 66.3) makes it clear that "memoirs of the apostles" and "gospels" are equivalent, and the use of the plural indicates Justin's awareness of more than one written gospel. ("The apostles in the memoirs which have come from them, which are also called gospels, have transmitted that the Lord had commanded...").[127] Justin may have preferred the designation "memoirs of the apostles" as a contrast to the "gospel" of his contemporary Marcion to emphasize the connections between the historical testimony of the gospels and the Old Testament prophecies which Marcion rejected.[128]

The origin of Justin's use the name "memoirs of the apostles" as a synonym for the gospels is uncertain.

---

[127] Koester (1990) Ancient Christian Gospels: Their History and Development pp. 38,40–41; p. 38 – Dial. 100.4; 101.3; 102.5; 103.6,8; 104.1; 105.1,5,6; 106.1,3,4; 107.1 "In each instance the materials quoted derive from written gospels, usually from Matthew and Luke, in one instance from Mark, and each time the term serves to quote, or to refer to, gospel materials which demonstrate that the prophecy of the Psalm has been fulfilled in the story of Jesus. The "memoirs of the apostles" are used as reliable historical records." p40 – "Justin uses the term gospel only three times 1 Apol. 66.3, Dial. 10.2; 100.1." p. 41 – "It is evident that "gospel" refers to the same literature that Justin otherwise calls "memoirs of the apostles". The use of the plural in 1 Apol. 66.3 indicates that Justin knew of more than one written gospel."

[128] Koester 1990 Ancient Christian Gospels: Their History and Development pp. 36–37,43; pp. 36–37 – "...there is no evidence that anyone before Marcion had used the term "gospel" as a designation for a written document. ...those writings of Justin which are preserved, his two Apologies and his Dialogue with Trypho, clearly show the effects of Marcion's challenge." p. 43 – "In direct antithesis to Marcion's use of the written gospel, Justin binds these gospels to the prophetic revelation in the Old Testament scriptures."

Scholar David E. Aune has argued that the gospels were modeled after classical Greco-Roman biographies, and Justin's use of the term apomnemoneumata to mean all the Synoptic Gospels should be understood as referring to a written biography such as the Memorabilia of Xenophon because they preserve the authentic teachings of Jesus.[129] However, scholar Helmut Koester has pointed out the Greek title "Memorabilia" was not applied to Xenophon's work until the Middle Ages, and it is more likely apomnemoneumata was used to describe the oral transmission of the sayings of Jesus in early Christianity. Papias uses a similar term meaning "remembered" (apomnemoneusen) when describing how Mark accurately recorded the "recollections of Peter", and Justin also uses it in reference to Peter in Dial. 106.3, followed by a quotation found only in the Gospel of Mark (Mk 3:16–17). Therefore, according to Koester, it is likely that Justin applied the name "memoirs of the apostles" analogously to indicate the trustworthy recollections of the apostles found in the written record of the Synoptic Gospels of Matthew, Mark, and Luke, and possibly also an apocryphal gospel.[130]

---

[129] Aune (1987) The New Testament in its Literary Environment p. 67 – "Justin Martyr (writing ca. 155) described the Gospels as 'reminiscences [apomnemoneumata] of the apostles' (1 Apology 66.3; 67.3) and 'reminiscences of Peter' (Dialogue with Trypho 106.3). Thus Justin, like Matthew, Luke, and Papias, prefers to designate the Gospels by a recognized literary form. Though apomnemoneumata are not carefully defined in rhetorical handbooks, they are essentially expanded chreiai, i.e., sayings and/or actions of or about specific individuals, set in a narrative framework and transmitted by memory (hence "reliable"). ... His use of the term "reminiscences", therefore, suggests a connection to Xenophon's Memorabilia (in Greek apomnemoneumata), a "biography" of Socrates."

[130] Koester 1990 Ancient Christian Gospels: Their History and Development pp. 33–34,38–40; pp. 33–34 – "What Papias says about

Justin expounded on the gospel texts as an accurate recording of the fulfillment of prophecy, which he combined with quotations of the prophets of Israel from the LXX to demonstrate a proof from prophecy of the Christian kerygma.[131] The importance which Justin attaches to the words of the prophets, which he regularly quotes with the formula "it is written", shows his estimate of the Old Testament Scriptures. However, the scriptural authority he attributes to the "memoirs of the apostles" is less certain. Koester articulates a majority view among scholars that Justin considered the "memoirs of the apostles" to be accurate historical records but not inspired writings,[132] whereas scholar Charles E. Hill, though

---

Mark reflects the use of categories which are drawn from the oral tradition. ... The written gospels' authority is assured by the same technical terms which had been established for the oral tradition. ... The term "remember" (mnemoneuein/apomnemoneuein) was decisive for the trustworthiness of the oral tradition." pp. 39–40 – "The composite form of the verb "to remember" (apomnemoneuein) had been used by Papias of Hierapolis as a technical term for the transmission of oral materials about Jesus. If Justin's term "memoirs of the apostles" is derived from this usage, it designates the written gospels as the true recollections of the apostles, trustworthy and accurate, and more reliable than any oral tradition which they are destined to replace."

[131] Koester 1990 Ancient Christian Gospels: Their History and Development p. 377 – "The Christian proclamation about Jesus as Son of God, however, is true (in contrast to pagan myths), because the Christians possess trustworthy historical documents – "remembrances of the apostles" – from which it can be shown that everything in Christ's appearance and work happened in complete agreement with prophecy. What is demonstrated to be true is the Christian kerygma, not the story of the gospels. The reports contained in the gospels are used to show that the facts about Christ which the kerygma proclaims happened in complete agreement with the prophecy that announced them."

[132] Koester 1990 Ancient Christian Gospels: Their History and Development p. 41 – "These gospels for Justin possess the authority of written records. Although they are read in the service of the church, they are not "Holy Scripture" like the law and the prophets."

acknowledging the position of mainstream scholarship, contends that Justin regarded the fulfillment quotations of the gospels to be equal in authority.[133]

Scriptural Sources

Gospels

Justin uses material from the Synoptic Gospels (Matthew, Mark, and Luke) in the composition of the First Apology and the Dialogue, either directly, as in the case of Matthew,[134] or indirectly through the use of a gospel harmony, which may have been composed by Justin or his school.[135] However, his use, or even knowledge, of the Gospel of John is uncertain. One possible reference to John is a saying that is quoted in the context of a description of Christian baptism (1 Apol. 61.4

---

[133] Hill (2004) pp. 345–46; p. 345 – "It is commonly held that in Rome of Justin's day even the Memoirs themselves possessed only a quite limited authority."; p. 346 – He sees in Justin "a parity of authority between these two groups of writings".

[134] Skarsaune (1987) The Proof From Prophecy pp. 130,163; p. 130 – "Justin sometimes had direct access to Matthew and quotes OT texts directly from him. ... (The direct borrowings are most frequent in the Dialogue; in the Apology, Mic 5:1 in 1 Apol. 34:1 may be the only instance.)" p. 163 note: Diagram of the internal structure of the putative "kerygma source", showing the insertion of scriptural quotation of Mic 5:1 from Mt. 2:6

[135] Koester, (2000) Introduction to the New Testament: History and literature of Early Christianity. 2nd ed., 1982 1st ed., p. 344 – "On the basis of the gospel quotations of the First Apology and the Dialogue with Trypho, one can conclude with great certainty that Justin also had composed a harmony of the Gospels of Matthew, Mark, and Luke (he did not know the Gospel of John), which is lost but was used by his student Tatian for the composition of his famous and influential four-gospel harmony known as the Diatessaron."

– "Unless you are reborn, you cannot enter into the kingdom of heaven."). However, Koester contends that Justin obtained this saying from a baptismal liturgy rather than a written gospel.[136]

Apocalypse

Justin does not quote from the Book of Revelation directly, yet he clearly refers to it, naming John as its author (Dial. 81.4 "Moreover also among us a man named John, one of the apostles of Christ, prophesied in a revelation made to him that those who have believed on our Christ will spend a thousand years in Jerusalem; and that hereafter the general and, in short, the eternal resurrection and judgment of all will likewise take place"). Scholar Brooke Westcott notes that this reference to the author of the single prophetic book of the New Testament illustrates the distinction Justin made between the role of prophecy and fulfillment quotations from the gospels, as Justin does not mention any of the individual canonical gospels by name.[137]

---

[136] Koester (1990) Ancient Christian Gospels pp. 360–361; p. 360 – "He knew and quoted especially the Gospels of Matthew and Luke; he must have known the Gospel of Mark as well, though there is only one explicit reference to this Gospel (Dial. 106.3); he apparently had no knowledge of the Gospel of John." footnote #2: "The only possible reference to the Gospel of John is the quotation of a saying in 1 Apol. 61.4.."

[137] Westcott (1875) A general survey of the canon of the New Testament, p. 120 – "To quote prophecy habitually without mentioning the Prophet's name would be to deprive it of half it's value; and if it seem strange that Justin does not quote the Evangelists like Prophets, it is no less worthy of notice that he does quote by name the single prophetic book of the New Testament. ... This reference to the Apocalypse appears to illustrate the difference which Justin makes between his quotations from the Prophecies and the Gospels."

Letters

Reflecting his opposition to Marcion, Justin's attitude toward the Pauline epistles generally corresponds to that of the later Church. In Justin's works, distinct references are found to Romans, 1 Corinthians, Galatians, Ephesians, Colossians, and 2 Thessalonians, and possible ones to Philippians, Titus, and 1 Timothy. It seems likely that he also knew Hebrews and 1 John. The apologetic character of Justin's habit of thought appears again in the Acts of his martyrdom, the genuineness of which is attested by internal evidence.[138]

Testimony Sources

According to scholar Oskar Skarsaune, Justin relies on two main sources for his proofs from prophecy that probably circulated as collections of scriptural testimonies within his Christian school. He refers to Justin's primary source for demonstrating scriptural proofs in the First Apology and parallel passages in the Dialogue as a "kerygma source". A second source, which was used only in the Dialogue, may be identical to a lost dialogue attributed to Aristo of Pella on the divine nature of the Messiah, the Dialogue of Jason and Papiscus (ca. 140). Justin brings in biblical quotes verbatim from these sources, and he often appears to be paraphrasing his sources very closely, even in his interpretive remarks.[139]

---

[138] Bonwetsch (1914) New Schaff–Herzog Encyclopedia of Religious Knowledge, p. 284; Also see, Martyrdom of Justin Martyr at Wikisource

[139] Skarsaune (2007) Jewish Believers in Jesus pp. 380–81

Justin occasionally uses the Gospel of Matthew directly as a source for Old Testament prophecies to supplement his testimony sources.[140] However, the fulfillment quotations from these sources most often appear to be harmonizations of the gospels of Matthew and Luke.[141] Koester suggests that Justin had composed an early harmony along the lines of his pupil Tatian's Diatesseron. However, the existence of a harmony independent of a collection of sayings for exposition purposes has been disputed by scholar Arthur Bellinzoni.[142] The question of whether the harmonized

---

[140] Skarsaune (1987) The Proof From Prophecy pp. 130,163; p. 130 – "Justin sometimes had direct access to Matthew and quotes OT texts directly from him. ... (The direct borrowings are most frequent in the Dialogue; in the Apology, Mic 5:1 in 1 Apol. 34:1 may be the only instance.)" p. 163 note: Diagram of the internal structure of the putative "kerygma source", showing the insertion of scriptural quotation of Mic 5:1 from Mt. 2:6 / Koester (1990) Ancient Christian Gospels pp. 382–383 – "In the discussion of the prophecy for the place of Jesus' birth (1 Apology 34), Justin only quotes the prophecy of Micah 5:1 and then remarks that Jesus was born in this 'village in the land of Judah which is 35 stades from Jerusalem' (1 Apol. 34:2). No actual narrative material from a gospel is quoted. ... However, the quotation of the text of Micah 5:1 is not given in the text of the LXX; rather, Justin follows the form of the text quoted in Matt. 2:6. ... The form of the quotation that appears in Matt 2:6 departs considerably from both the LXX and the Hebrew text. It is, in fact, a combination of Micah 5:1 and 2 Sam 5:2; only the latter speaks of the prince's function as the Shepard of Israel. The conflated quotation was wholly the work of Matthew. There can be no question that Justin is quoting this Matthean text."

[141] Koester (1990) Ancient Christian Gospels p. 365 – "The vast majority of the sayings quoted in Justin's writings are harmonizations of the texts of Matthew and Luke. These harmonizations are not casual or accidental, but systematic and consistent, (this certainly excludes...careless quotation from memory as an explanation for Justin's harmonizations) and they involve the composition of longer sections of parallel sayings from both gospels."

[142] Bellinzoni (1967) Sayings of Jesus in Justin Martyr p. 141 – "It must, however, be emphasized that there is absolutely no evidence that Justin

gospel materials found in Justin's writings came from a preexisting gospel harmony or were assembled as part of an integral process of creating scriptural proof texts is an ongoing subject of scholarly investigation.[143]

The "Kerygma Source"

The following excerpt from 1 Apol. 33:1,4–5 (partial parallel in Dial. 84) on the annunciation and virgin birth of Jesus shows how Justin used harmonized gospel verses from Matthew and Luke to provide a scriptural proof of

---

ever composed a complete harmony of the synoptic gospels; his harmonies were of limited scope and were apparently composed for didactic purposes. Whether the thought of a full gospel harmony ever occurred to Justin can only be conjectured, but he apparently never undertook to compose such a work." / Koester (1990) The Ancient Christian Gospels p. 370 footnote 2: "Bellinzoni (Sayings of Jesus in Justin Martyr p. 100) collapses stage (1) [a systematic harmonization of the texts of Matthew and Luke] and (2) [the composition of a cluster of sayings that warn against false prophets] of this process. He assumes that the harmonizations were made specifically for the composition of a catechism. This assumption, however, cannot explain why also the narrative materials quoted by Justin were drawn from a harmonized gospel text."

[143] Koester (1990) Ancient Christian Gospels p. 378 – "The question is whether Justin composed these harmonizations and inserted additional phrases just for the purpose of his demonstration of scriptural proof or whether he drew on a written gospel text that was already harmonized and expanded. It seems to me that we are not witnessing the work of an apologist who randomly selects pieces of various gospels and invents additional phrases for the purpose of a tight argument of literal fulfillment of scripture; nor can one solve the complex problems of Justin's quotations of gospel narrative materials by the hypothesis of a ready-made, established text of a harmonized gospel as his source. Rather, his writings permit insights into a school of scriptural exegesis in which careful comparison of written gospels with the prophecies of scripture endeavored to produce an even more comprehensive new gospel text."

the messiah-ship of Jesus based on fulfillment of the prophecy of Isaiah 7:14.[144]

> "And hear again how Isaiah in express words foretold that He should be born of a virgin; for he spoke thus: 'Behold, the virgin will conceive in the womb and bear a son, and they will say in his name, God with us' (Mt 1:23)." (1 Apol. 33:1)[145]

> "...the power of God, coming down upon the virgin, overshadowed her and made her while yet a virgin to conceive (cf. Lk 1:35), and the angel of God proclaimed to her and said, 'Behold, you will conceive in the womb from the Holy Spirit and bear a son (Mt 1:20/Lk 1:31) and he will be called Son of the Most High (Lk 1:32). And you shall call his name Jesus, because he will save his people from their sins (Mt 1:21),' as those who have made memoirs of

---

[144] Skarsaune (1987) The Proof From Prophecy p. 145 – "1 Apol. 33 contains an elaborate explanation of Is 7:14. ... One notices that the fulfillment report is stylized so as to match the prophecy perfectly. That Justin did not entirely formulate it ad hoc is demonstrated by the close parallel in the Proteuangelium Iakobi (PJ 11:3), where much of the same combination of Matthean and Lukan elements occurs. Probably all three elements (Prophecy – Exposition – Fulfillment report) were present in Justin's source. And – as pointed out by Koester [Koester (1956) p. 67] – it seems the same source is employed once more in Dial. 84."

[145] Koester (1990) Ancient Christian Gospels p. 379 – "1 Apol. 33 gives as proof concerning Jesus' birth the prophecy of Isa 7:14. The text of this scriptural passage is presented in a form that is influenced by its quotation in Matt 1:23." / Skarsaune (1987) The Proof From Prophecy pp. 32–34; p. 32 – "It is obvious that Justin's quotation of IS 7:14 in 1 Apol. 33:1 has Mt 1:23 as its direct or indirect source.

all things about our savior Jesus Christ taught...
(1 Apol. 33:4–5)[146]

According to Skarsaune, the harmonized gospel narratives of Matthew and Luke were part of a tradition already circulating within Justin's school that expounded on the life and work of Jesus as the Messiah and the apostolic mission. Justin then rearranged and expanded these testimonia to create his First Apology.[147] The

---

[146] Koester (1990) Ancient Christian Gospels pp. 380–81 – "The text of 1 Apol. 33:5 is a harmony of two angelic announcements, the one from Matthew in which the angel calls Joseph in a dream, the other from Luke's narrative of the annunciation. While the passage begins with a sentence from Luke, 'from the Holy Spirit' is interpolated from Matt 1:20. The naming of Jesus and the reason for this name is given according to Matt 1:21. ... But in order to argue for the fulfillment of Isa 7:14 in 1 Apol. 33:3–6, the report of the command to name the child 'Jesus' did not need to refer to the Matthean form. ... It is evident, therefore, that Justin is quoting from a harmonized gospel text... Justin's gospel text must have continued with the remainder of the Lukan pericope of the annunciation. In the introduction to the harmonization of Luke 1:31–32 and Matt 1:20–21, Justin had already alluded to the Lukan continuation of the story: 1 Apol. 33:4 ... recalls Luke 1:35 ("The Holy Spirit will come upon you and the power of the Most High will overshadow you.")

[147] Skarsaune (1987) The Proof From Prophecy pp. 143,425; p. 143 – "Taking as a working hypothesis that Justin in 1 Apol. 32/35 and Dial. 52–54 is using a source containing OT prophecies, expositions and fulfillment reports, it is easy to recognize the different procedure in the Apology and the Dialogue. In the Apology, Justin reproduces the source rather faithfully, only rearranging the material... In the Dialogue Justin is much more independent in his handling of his (kerygma) source. He has turned to the primary sources behind the testimony source, that is, he has turned to the LXX and Matthew." p. 425 – "The prooftexts themselves were presented in a free, targumizing version of the standard LXX text, closely adapted to Christian exegesis and polemic concerns. ... Justin may have become heir to Schriftbeweistraktate which were part of a school tradition. These tracts probably also comprised brief fulfillment reports. We encounter this tradition of texts and exposition in its purest form in 1 Apol. 31–53. Here Justin is still almost entirely dependent on the received texts and the adjacent exegesis. ...

"kerygma source" of prooftexts (contained within 1 Apol. 31–53) is believed to have had a Two Parousias Christology, characterized by the belief that Jesus first came in humility, in fulfillment of prophecy, and will return in glory as the Messiah to the Gentiles.[148] There are close literary parallels between the Christology of Justin's source and the Apocalypse of Peter.[149]

Dialogue of Jason and Papiscus

The following excerpts from the Dialogue with Trypho of the baptism (Dial. 88:3,8) and temptation (Dial. 103:5–6) of Jesus, which are believed to have originated from the Dialogue of Jason and Papiscus, illustrate the use of gospel narratives and sayings of Jesus

---

Justin's main modification is a rearrangement within the series, motivated by Justin's fear that his readers might not recognize some of his prooftexts as real prophecies." / Skarsaune (2007) Jewish Believers in Jesus pp. 381–85; p. 381 – "The reason I have called this hypothetical source the "kerygma source" is twofold. First, it share some striking parallels with the lost writing The Kerygma of Peter (ca. 125) of which a few fragments are quoted in Clement of Alexandria. Second, it seems to have had a creed-like enumeration of Jesus' messianic career, a christological "kerygma", as its basic structure.

[148] karsaune (1987) The Proof From Prophecy pp. 154–56; p. 156 – "In the Apology, the idea is the following: Since the prophecies covering the first coming of Christ can be shown to have been fulfilled in great detail, we may safely conclude that those prophecies which predict His glorious second coming will also be fulfilled."

[149] Skarsaune (2007) Jewish Believers in Jesus pp. 388–9 – "The Christology is clearly messianic in function: the 'Son of God' concept is demonstrated functionally as the Messiah being enthroned at God's right hand, ruling, and coming to judge the living and the dead, thus acting in a divine role. On the whole, this Christology is very close to that of Matthew, but also to the Christology of Justin's source in 1 Apol. 31–53.

in a testimony source and how Justin has adopted these "memoirs of the apostles" for his own purposes.

> "And then, when Jesus had come to the river Jordan where John was baptizing, and when Jesus came down into the water, a fire was even kindled in the Jordan, and when He was rising up from the water, the Holy Spirit fluttered down upon Him in the form of a dove, as the apostles have written about this very Christ of ours." (Dial. 88:3)

> "And when Jesus came to the Jordan, and being supposed to be the son of Joseph the carpenter..., the Holy Spirit, and for man's sake, as I said before, fluttered down upon Him, and a voice came at the time out of the heavens – which was spoken also by David, when he said, impersonating Christ, what the Father was going to say to Him – 'You are My Son, this day I have begotten you'." (Dial. 88:8)[150]

"...the Devil himself,...[was] called serpent by Moses, the Devil by Job and Zachariah, and was addressed as

---

[150] Skarsaune (1987) The Proof From Prophecy pp. 197–198,391–392; p. 197 – "Justin's narrative is a harmonization of the Synoptic accounts. There are other non-synoptic details in the context, however, which may indicate a non-synoptic source besides the Synoptic Gospels." pp. 391–392 – "I have argued above that the narrative of Jesus' baptism in Dial. 88:3 derives from the "recapitulation" source. ... Men believed that Jesus was the son of Joseph, but the heavenly voice proclaimed him as God's son. Perhaps the mention of the fire is related to this idea: It may have been conceived of as a purifying or testing fire. ... Jesus at his baptism was tested as God's son by the fire, but not made God's son at his baptism. This, I gather, is also the idea embodied in Justin's narrative: Jesus was not made or established as God's son in his baptism, but he was proved to be God's son – proved by testing, or by conquering the fire."

Satanas by Jesus. This indicated that he had a compound name made up of the actions which he performed; for the word "Sata" in the Hebrew and Syrian tongue means "apostate", while "nas" is the word which means in translation "serpent", thus, from both parts is formed the one word "Sata-nas". It is narrated in the memoirs of the apostles that as soon as Jesus came up out of the river Jordan and a voice said to him: 'You are My Son, this day I have begotten you', this Devil came and tempted him, even so far as to exclaim: 'Worship me'; but Christ replied: 'Get behind me, Satanas, the Lord your God shall you worship, and Him only shall you serve'. For, since the Devil had deceived Adam, he fancied that he could in some way harm him also." (Dial. 103:5–6)[151]

The quotations refer to the fulfillment of a prophecy of Psalm 2:7 found in the Western text-type of Luke 3:22.[152] Justin's mention of the fire on the Jordan

---

[151] Skarsaune (1987) The Proof From Prophecy pp. 222–23,238,383–84,393; p. 384 – "In the temptation story, Christ as the Son of God, the second Adam, is tested. The temptation follows immediately after the heavenly voice has proclaimed 'Thou art my son...'. This is especially clear in Dial. 103:5f. ... The special relevance of this passage is that it proves how deeply the recapitulation idea is integrated into Justin's inherited material. The etymology given for Satanas has a special function: It proves that the 'Satanas' encountered by Jesus in his temptation was the same as the 'serpent' encountered by Adam – Satanas means 'apostate serpent', i.e. the serpent of Gen. 3. In other words: Jesus met the same adversary as the first Adam." p. 393 – "It is interesting to notice that only two Semitic etymologies provided by Justin both refer to the temptation story: 'Satanas' and 'Israel' (Dial. 103:5 and Dial. 125:4) – and as we have seen already, they presuppose a harmonistic version of the temptation story which is not created ad hoc by Justin. The gist of the whole material is succinctly summarized in Dial. 103:6: As the devil led Adam astray, he thought he could seduce the second Adam also."

[152] Koester (1990) Ancients Christians Gospels pp. 394–395 – "In Dial. 88, Justin twice reports the coming of the holy spirit upon Jesus at his

without comment suggests that he was relying on an intermediate source for these gospel quotations,[153] and his literal interpretation of a pseudo-etymology of the Hebrew word Satan indicates a dependence on a testimony source with a knowledge of Hebrew, which was probably the Dialogue of Jason and Papiscus.[154]

---

baptism. He gives this report in order to demonstrate the fulfillment of the prophecies of Isa 11:1–3 and Joel 2:28–29 about the coming of the spirit which he had quoted in Dial. 87:2 and 6. ... Finally, the heavenly voice is given by Justin in a citation of Ps. 2:7, while Mark and Matthew present a wording of the heavenly voice which is a conflation of Isa 42:1 and 44:2. Only the Western text of Luke 3:22 presents the heavenly voice in the form that must be presupposed for Justin's source. Justin cannot have been the author of this form of the heavenly voice; he had no special interest in proving the fulfillment of this scriptural text, although he is quite aware of its appearance in scripture as a word of David, i.e., a psalm that David wrote. That Justin's source already contained this form of the heavenly voice is confirmed in Dial. 103:6, where he refers to it once more in passing; introducing a remark about Jesus' temptation, he again quotes the exact text of Luke 3:22 D = Ps. 2:7."

[153] Koester (1990) Ancients Christians Gospels p. 395 – "In order to prove the fulfillment of the prophecies of Isa 11:1–3 and Joel 2:28–29, Justin only had to report the coming of the spirit upon Jesus. But not only does he add the report about the heavenly voice, he also mentions 'that a fire was lit in the Jordan'. Nothing in the context of Justin's discussion requires a mention of this phenomenon. It must have been part of the text Justin was quoting."

[154] Rokeah (2002) Justin Martyr and the Jews pp. 20–21 – "The accepted view is that Justin did not know Hebrew. There is clear-cut and overwhelming evidence for Justin's absolute reliance upon the Septuagint. The explanation for any apparent acquaintance or knowledge of Hebrew in Justin's writings should be sought elsewhere: in his sources. ... Dial. 103:5 contains the only two Hebrew–Aramaic etymologies in the entire work: of satan, and of yisrael. The source of these is apparently the work of Aristo of Pella, The Altercation of Jason and Papiscus."

The Dialogue attributed to Aristo of Pella is believed to have furnished Justin with scriptural prooftexts on the divinity of the Messiah by combining a Wisdom Christology – Christ as the incarnation of preexistent Wisdom – with a Second Adam Christology – the first Adam was conquered by Satan, but this Fall of Man is reversed by Christ as the Second Adam who conquers Satan. This is implied in the pseudo-etymology in Dial. 103:5–6 linking the name of Satan to the "apostate-serpent". The Christology of the source is close to that of the Ascension of Isaiah.[155]

Catechal Sources

Justin quotes many sayings of Jesus in 1 Apol. 15–17 and smaller sayings clusters in Dial. 17:3–4; 35:3; 51:2–3; and 76:4–7. The sayings are most often harmonizations of Matthew and Luke that appear to be grouped together topically and organized into sayings collections, including

---

[155] Skarsaune (2007) Jewish Believers in Jesus pp. 399–400; "In Justin's source, the Messiah is presented as God's preexistent Wisdom who has descended to earth, and ascended again to his heavenly glory. ... Here I add another aspect of great significance in Justin's source, namely that Jesus is portrayed as the second and anti-typical Adam. He reverses the fall of Adam by conquering where Adam was conquered. He "recapitulates" in his own story the story of Adam, but with the opposite point of departure, the opposite direction and the opposite result. ... The very point of the (pseudo-)etymology given for Satanas in this passage is to identify the Tempter addressed by Jesus in Matt 4:11 (conflated with Matt 16:23) with the serpent that tempted the first man. In this way the parallelism between the first and second Adam is made plain. Since Justin knew no Hebrew and probably no Aramaic, there is every reason to think he got this midrashic etymology from a source..."

material that probably originated from an early Christian catechism.[156]

The following example of an ethical teaching On Swearing Oaths in 1 Apol. 16:5 shows a combination of sayings material found in Matthew and the Epistle of James:

"Do not swear at all (Mt 5:34). Let your Yes be Yes and your No be No (Jas 5:12). Everything beyond these is from evil (Mt 5:37)."

The saying "Let your Yes be Yes and your No be No" from James 5:12 is interpolated into a sayings complex from Matthew 5:34,37. The text appears in a large number of Patristic quotations and twice in the Clementine Homilies (Hom. 3:55, 19:2). Thus, it is likely that Justin was quoting this harmonized text from a catechism.[157]

---

[156] Koester (1990) Ancient Christian Gospels p. 361 – "The most striking feature is that these sayings exhibit many harmonizations of the text of Matthew and Luke. However, the simple assumption of a harmonized gospel cannot explain all the peculiarities of the quotations." / Bellinzoni (1967) Sayings of Jesus in Justin Martyr pp. 99–100 – "It has already been argued above that the entire section Apol. 15–17 may have been based on a single source different from the sources underlying the rest of Justin's sayings of Jesus, and I have tried to indicate that this section has many features in common with primitive Christian catechisms."

[157] Bellinzoni (1967) Sayings of Jesus in Justin Martyr pp. 64–67; p. 66 – "the form of the saying in James is a more simple paranetic form than the text of Matthew, where each example is elaborated and where the command is not what one should do but what one should say. It, therefore, appears that the form of the saying in Jas. 5:12 is older than Matthew's version. ... This evidence would seem to indicate that Apol. 16:5 was here based on the text of Mt. 5:34,37 that had either been harmonized in part with Jas. 5:12 or with the parenetic tradition that underlies Jas. 5:12. The evidence of several of the fathers indicates a widespread knowledge of a text similar to Apol. 16:5." (Clem. of Alex. Strom. V 14,99; Clem. of Alex. Strom. VII 11,67; Cyril of Alex. De Ador.

The harmonization of Matthew and Luke is evident in the following quotations of Mt 7:22–23 and Lk 13:26–27, which are used by Justin twice, in 1 Apol. 16:11 and Dial. 76:5:

> "Many will say to me, 'Lord, Lord, did we not in your name eat and drink and do powerful deeds?' And then I shall say to them, 'go away from me, workers of lawlessness'."

> "Many will say to me on that day, 'Lord, Lord, did we not in your name eat and drink and prophecy and drive out demons?' And I shall say to them, 'go away from me'."

In both cases, Justin is using the same harmonized text of Matthew and Luke, although neither of the quotations includes the entire text of those gospel passages. The last phrase, "workers of lawlessness", has an exact parallel with 2 Clement 4:5. This harmonized text also appears in a large number of quotations by the Church Fathers.[158] 1 Apol. 16:11 is part of a larger unit of

---

et Verit. VI; Eusebius Dem. Ev. III 3,13; Eusebius Comm. in Ps. 14 4; Epiphanius Adv. Her. XIX 6,21; Gregory of Nyssa In Cant. of Cant. Homily XIII) / Koester (1990) Ancient Christian Gospels p. 363 – "Thus...it is not likely that Justin is quoting from the text of Matthew but from a catechism, whose text was influenced by the formulation preserved in Jas 5:12 but not necessarily dependent upon the Epistle of James."

[158] Koester (1990) Ancient Christian Gospels pp. 356,365–67; p. 367 – "The method of harmonization includes two different procedures: (1) whenever the texts of Matthew and Luke are closely parallel, either the Matthean or the Lukan phrase or a conflation of both is chosen; (2) whenever the texts of Matthew and Luke differ considerably, as in Matt 7:22 and Luke 13:26, major portions of the two texts are combined; thus, one finds Luke's 'we were eating and drinking' as well as Matthew's 'we prophesied etc.'." / Bellinzoni (1967) Sayings of Jesus in Justin Martyr pp. 22–25; pp. 24–25 – "These consistent features of harmonization found in Apol. 16:11 and Dial. 76:5 leave little doubt

sayings material in 1 Apol 16:9–13 which combines a warning against being unprepared with a warning against false prophets. The entire unit is a carefully composed harmony of parallel texts from Matthew and Luke.[159] This unit is part of a larger collection of sayings found in 1 Apol. 15–17 that appear to have originated from a catechism used by Justin's school in Rome, which may have had a wide circulation. Justin excerpted and rearranged the catechetical sayings material to create Apol. 15–17 and parallel passages in the Dialogue.[160]

---

that Justin used as a source for these passages a written harmony of Mt. 7:22f and Lk. 13:26f, and this harmonization of Matthew and Luke is further evident in several of the early fathers quoted in the texts below. ... A comparison of this harmonization of Matthew and Luke in the patristic quotations leaves little doubt that Justin used a harmony of Mt. 7:22f and Lk. 13:26f and that this harmony was known to other fathers in substantially the same form as that used by Justin (Origen Contra Celsum II 49; Origen Ev. Jo. XXXII 8,11; Pamphilius Apol. pro Orig. V). Further, the witness of 2 Clement here proves the existence of this harmonization of Matthew and Luke previous to Justin."

[159] Bellinzoni (1967) Sayings of Jesus in Justin Martyr pp. 98–99; p. 99 – "Therefore we can conclude with certainty that these five verses are based on a source that was a carefully composed harmony of material from Matthew and Luke and that was based on the order of Matthew 7." / Koester (1990) Ancient Christian Gospels pp. 367–370; p. 369 – "This section of Justin's quotation of Jesus' sayings rests on deliberate and careful composition of the parallel texts of Matthew and Luke, but is also disrupted by interpolations from different contexts." p. 370 – "Thus Justin himself did not compose this cluster of sayings for this particular context. He use an already existing collection."

[160] Bellinzoni (1967) Sayings of Jesus in Justin Martyr p. 100 – "It is, therefore, quite probable from the foregoing discussion that there is underlying Apol. 15–17 a primitive Christian catechism in use in Justin's school in Rome, a catechism that was known in similar form to Clement of Alexandria, Origen, and the author of the Pseudo-Clementine Homilies, a catechism based primarily on the text of the Sermon on the Mount but that harmonized related material from Mark, Luke, and

Other Sources

Justin includes a tract on Greek mythology in 1 Apol. 54 and Dial. 69 which asserts that myths about various pagan deities are imitations of the prophecies about Christ in the Old Testament. There is also a small tract in 1 Apol. 59–60 on borrowings of the philosophers from Moses, particularly Plato. These two tracts may be from the same source, which may have been an early Christian Apology.[161]

---

from other parts of Matthew, and a catechism whose tradition was of great influence in later manuscript witnesses of the synoptic gospels."

Koester (1990) Ancient Christian Gospels p. 375 – "The catechetical character of these clusters of sayings is evident in their usage by Justin ... It is difficult to determine in each instance the degree to which Justin has supplemented and rearranged these collections. But it appears that the catechetical collections already existed and that Justin himself did not compose them."

[161] Skarsaune (1987) The Proof From Prophecy pp. 52–53,148–150,431; p. 150 – "This tract must have had a somewhat other orientation than the source employed by Justin in 1 Apol. 32–35. It was not concerned with a prophecy–fulfillment scheme, but with correspondence between OT texts and Greek mythology." p. 53 – "It is unlikely that it (the text in 1 Apol. 60:9 introduced as a prophecy of Moses) ever occurred in a Bible text...it is more likely that Justin took it from the source which also provided him with the (harmonistic) 'citations' from Plato in A 60. ... In this case we have reason to suspect a tractate of some kind, which included Plato quotations as well." p. 431 – "It remains to be remarked that Justin also has made other additions from sources containing OT material, but these are strictly speaking not parts of the scriptural proof. In 1 Apol. 54f and Dial. 69f Justin has added material from a source which was occupied with demonic imitations of OT Messianic prophecies, and in 1 Apol. 59f he has a little tract on philosophic borrowings from Moses. One should not exclude the possibility that these two blocks of material derive from the same source, which might well be an earlier Christian Apology."

Prophetic Exegesis

Belief in Prophecy

The truth of the prophets, he declares, compels assent. The Old Testament is an inspired guide and counselor. He puts the following words in the mouth of the Christian philosopher who converted him:

" 'There existed, long before this time, certain men more ancient than all those who are esteemed philosophers, both righteous and beloved by God, who spoke by the Divine Spirit, and foretold events which would take place, and which are now taking place. They are called prophets. These alone both saw and announced the truth to men, neither reverencing nor fearing any man. not influenced by a desire for glory, but speaking those things alone which they saw and which they heard, being filled with the Holy Spirit. Their writings are still extant, and he who has read them is very much helped in his knowledge of the beginning and end of things. . . And those events which have happened, and those which are happening, compel you to assent to the utterances made by them.'"[162]

Then Justin tells of his own experience:

"Straightway a flame was kindled in my soul; and a love of the prophets, and of those men who are friends of Christ, possessed me; and whilst revolving his words in my mind, I found this philosophy alone to be safe and profitable."[163]

---

[162] Dialogue with Trypho, Chapter 7

[163] Dialogue with Trypho, Chapter 8

Fulfillment

Justin talks of the following fulfillments of Bible prophecy

- The prophecies concerning the Messiah, and the particulars of His life.[164]
- The destruction of Jerusalem.[165]
- The Gentiles accepting Christianity.[166]
- Isaiah predicted that Jesus would be born of a virgin.[167]
- Micah mentions Bethlehem as the place of His birth.[168]
- Zechariah forecasts His entry into Jerusalem on the foal of an ass.[169]
- Second coming and Daniel 7[edit]
- Justin connects Christ's second coming with the climax of the prophecy of Daniel 7.

"But if so great a power is shown to have followed and to be still following the dispensation of His suffering, how great shall that be which shall follow His glorious advent! For He shall come on the clouds as the Son of man, so Daniel foretold, and His angels shall

---

[164] First Apology, Chapter 31

[165] First Apology, chapter 47

[166] First Apology, chapter 49

[167] First Apology, chapter 33

[168] First Apology, chapter 34

[169] First Apology, chapter 35

come with Him." [Then follows Dan. 7:9-28.][170]

Antichrist

The second glorious advent Justin places, moreover, close upon the heels of the appearance of the Antichrist, or "man of apostasy."[171] Justin's interpretation of prophecy is, however, less clear and full than that of others who follow.

Time, Times, and a Half

Daniel's "time, times, and a half", Justin believed, was nearing its consummation, when Antichrist would speak his blasphemies against the Most High. And he contends with Trypho over the meaning of a "time" and "times". Justin expects the time to be very short, but Trypho disagrees.

"The times now running on to their consummation; and he whom Daniel foretells would have dominion for a time, and times, and an half, is even already at the door, about to speak blasphemous and daring things against the Most High. But you, being ignorant of how long he will have dominion, hold another opinion. For you interpret the 'time' as being a hundred years. But if this is so, the man of sin must, at the shortest, reign three hundred and fifty years, in order that we may compute that which is said by the holy Daniel--'and times'--to be two times only."[172]

---

[170] Dailogue with Trypho, chapter 31

[171] Dailogue with Trypho, chapter 110

[172] Dailogue with Trypho, chapter 32

Eucharist

Justin's statements in his First Apology are some of the earliest Christian expressions on the Eucharist.

> "And this food is called among us [the Eucharist] ... For not as common bread and common drink do we receive these; but in like manner as Jesus Christ our Saviour, having been made flesh by the Word of God, had both flesh and blood for our salvation, so likewise have we been taught that the food which is blessed by the prayer of His word, and from which our blood and flesh by transmutation are nourished, is the flesh and blood of that Jesus who was made flesh." [173]

---

[173] First Apology, Chapter LXVI

CHAPTER 8 Tatian the Assyrian

Tatian the Assyrian[174] (c. 120–180 C.E.) was an Assyrian early Christian writer and theologian of the 2nd century.

Tatian's most influential work is the Diatessaron, a Biblical paraphrase, or "harmony", of the four gospels that became the standard text of the four gospels in the Syriac-speaking churches until the 5th-century, when it gave way to the four separate gospels in the Peshitta version.[175]

Life and Ministry

Concerning the date and place of his birth, little is known beyond what he tells about himself in his Oratio ad Graecos, chap. xlii (Ante-Nicene Fathers, ii. 81–82): that he was born in "the land of the Assyrians"; current scholarly consensus is that he died c. 185 AD, perhaps in Assyria.

He came to Rome, where he seems to have remained for some time. Here he seems to have for the first time encountered Christianity. According to his own representation, it was primarily his abhorrence of the pagan cults that led him to spend thought on religious problems. By the Old Testament, he says, he was

---

[174] http://en.wikipedia.org/wiki/Tatian

[175] Cross, F. L., ed. The Oxford Dictionary of the Christian Church. New York: Oxford University Press. 2005, articles Diatessaron and Peshitta

convinced of the unreasonableness of paganism. He adopted the Christian religion and became the pupil of Justin Martyr. It was the period when Christian philosophers competed with Greek sophists, and like Justin, he opened a Christian school in Rome. It is not known how long he labored in Rome without being disturbed.

Following the death of Justin in 165 AD, the life of Tatian is to some extent obscure. Irenaeus remarks (Haer., I., xxvlii. 1, Ante-Nicene Fathers, i. 353) that after the death of Justin, he was expelled from the church for his Encratitic (ascetic) views (Eusebius claims he founded the Encratitic sect), as well as for being a follower of the gnostic leader Valentinius. It is clear that Tatian left Rome, perhaps to reside for a while in either Greece or Alexandria, where he may have taught Clement.[citation needed] Epiphanius relates that Tatian established a school in Mesopotamia, the influence of which extended to Antioch in Syria, and was felt in Cilicia and especially in Pisidia.

The ascetic character which Syriac Christianity bore as late as the time of Aphraates was not impressed upon it by Tatian, but has roots that reach deeper.

The early development of the Syrian church furnishes a commentary on the attitude of Tatian in practical life. Thus for Aphraates baptism conditions the taking of a vow in which the catechumen promises celibacy. This shows how firmly the views of Tatian were established in Syria, and it supports the supposition that Tatian was the missionary of the countries around the Euphrates.

Writings

His Oratio ad Graecos (Address to the Greeks) condemns paganism as worthless, and praises the reasonableness and high antiquity of Christianity. As early as Eusebius, Tatian was praised for his discussions of the antiquity of Moses and of Jewish legislation, and it was because of this chronological section that his Oratio was not generally condemned.

His other major work was the Diatessaron, a "harmony" or synthesis of the four New Testament Gospels into a combined narrative of the life of Jesus. Ephrem the Syrian referred to it as the Evangelion da Mehallete ("The Gospel of the Mixed"), and it was practically the only gospel text used in Syria during the 3rd and 4th centuries.

In the 5th century the Diatessaron was replaced in those Syrian churches that used it by the four original Gospels. Rabbula, Bishop of Edessa, ordered the priests and deacons to see that every church should have a copy of the separate Gospels (Evangelion da Mepharreshe), and Theodoret, Bishop of Cyrus, removed more than two hundred copies of the Diatessaron from the churches in his diocese.

A number of recensions of the Diatessaron are available. The earliest, part of the Eastern family of recensions, is preserved in Ephraim's Commentary on Tatian's work, which itself is preserved in two versions: an Armenian translation preserved in two copies, and a copy of Ephraem's original Syriac text from the late 5th/early 6th century, which has been edited by Louis Lelow (Paris, 1966). Other translations include translations made into Arabic, Persian, and Old Georgian. A fragment of a narrative about the Passion found in the ruins of Dura-Europos in 1933 was once thought to have been from the Diatessaron, but more recent scholarly judgement does not connect it directly to Tatian's work.

The earliest member of the Western family of recensions is the Latin Codex Fuldensis, written at the request of bishop Victor of Capua in 545 AD. Although the text is clearly dependent on the Vulgate, the order of the passages is distinctly how Tatian arranged them. Tatian's influence can be detected much earlier in such Latin manuscripts as the Old Latin translation of the Bible, in Novatian's surviving writings, and in the Roman Antiphony. After the Codex Fuldensis, it would appear that members of the Western family lead an underground existence, popping into view over the centuries in an Old High German translation (c. 830), a Dutch (c. 1280), a Venetian manuscript of the 13th century, and a Middle English manuscript from 1400 that was once owned by Samuel Pepys.

In a lost writing, entitled On Perfection according to the Doctrine of the Savior, Tatian designates matrimony as a symbol of the tying of the flesh to the perishable world and ascribed the "invention" of matrimony to the devil. He distinguishes between the old and the new man; the old man is the law, the new man the Gospel. Other lost writings of Tatian include a work written before the Oratio ad Graecos that contrasts the nature of man with the nature of the animals, and a Problematon biblion which aimed to present a compilation of obscure Scripture sayings.

Theology

The starting-point of Tatian's theology is a strict monotheism which becomes the source of the moral life.

Originally the human soul possessed faith in one God, but lost it with the fall. In consequence, man sank under the rule of demons into the abominable error of polytheism. By monotheistic faith the soul is delivered from the material world and from demonic rule and is united with God. God is spirit (pneuma), but not the physical or stoical pneuma; he was alone before the creation, but he had within himself potentially the whole creation. Some scholars consider Tatian's creation theology as the beginning of teaching "ex nihilo" (creation from "nothing").[176]

The means of creation was the dynamis logike ("power expressed in words"). At first there proceeded from God the Logos who, generated in the beginning, was to produce the world by creating matter from which the whole creation sprang. Creation is penetrated by the *pneuma hylikon*, "world spirit," which is common to angels, stars, men, animals, and plants. This world spirit is lower than the divine pneuma, and becomes in man the psyche or "soul," so that on the material side and in his soul man does not differ essentially from the animals; though at the same time he is called to a peculiar union with the divine spirit, which raises him above the animals. This spirit is the image of God in man, and to it man's immortality is due.

The first-born of the spirits fell and caused others to fall, and thus the demons originated. The fall of the spirits was brought about through their desire to separate man from God, in order that he might serve not God but

---

[176] Edwin Hatch, The Influence of Greek Ideas and Usages upon the Christian Church, 195–196. The basis of the theory [ex nihilo] was Platonic, though some of the terms were borrowed from both Aristotle and the Stoics. It became itself the basis for the theory which ultimately prevailed in the Church. The transition appears in Tatian [ca. 170 A.D.

them. Man, however, was implicated in this fall, lost his blessed abode and his soul was deserted by the divine spirit, and sank into the material sphere, in which only a faint reminiscence of God remained alive.

As by freedom man fell, so by freedom he may turn again to God. The Spirit unites with the souls of those who walk uprightly; through the prophets he reminds men of their lost likeness to God. Although Tatian does not mention the name of Jesus, his doctrine of redemption culminates in his Christology.

CHAPTER 9 Athenagoras of Athens

Athenagoras (ca. 133 – 190 C.E.)[177] was a Father of the Church, an Ante-Nicene Christian apologist who lived during the second half of the 2nd century of whom little is known for certain, besides that he was Athenian (though possibly not originally from Athens), a philosopher, and a convert to Christianity. In his writings he styles himself as "Athenagoras, the Athenian, Philosopher, and Christian". There is some evidence that he was a Platonist before his conversion, but this is not certain.

Athenagoras' feast day is observed on 24 July in the Eastern Orthodox Church.

Work and writings

Although his work appears to have been well-known and influential, mention of him by other early Christian apologists, notably in the extensive writings of Eusebius, is strangely absent. It may be that his treatises, circulating anonymously, were for a time considered as the work of another apologist, or there may have been other circumstances now lost. There are only two mentions of him in early Christian literature: several accredited quotations from his Apology in a fragment of Methodius of Olympus (died 312) and some untrustworthy biographical details in the fragments of the Christian History of Philip of Side (c. 425). Philip of Side

---

[177] http://en.wikipedia.org/wiki/Athenagoras_of_Athens

claims that Athenagoras headed the Catechetical School of Alexandria (which is probably incorrect) and notes that Athenagoras converted to Christianity after initially familiarizing himself with the Scriptures in an attempt to controvert them.

His writings bear witness to his erudition and culture, his power as a philosopher and rhetorician, his keen appreciation of the intellectual temper of his age, and his tact and delicacy in dealing with the powerful opponents of his religion. Thus his writings are credited by some later scholars as having had a more significant impact on their intended audience than the now better-known writings of his more polemical and religiously-grounded contemporaries.

Of his writings, of which there were likely many, there have been preserved but a few: his Embassy for the Christians (often referred to the Apology), and a treatise titled the Resurrection of the Dead aka On the Resurrection of the Body.

The Embassy for the Christians, the date of which is fixed by internal evidence as late in 176 or 177, was a carefully written plea for justice to the Christians made by a philosopher, on philosophical grounds, to the Emperors Marcus Aurelius and his son Commodus, whom he flatters as conquerors, "but above all, philosophers". He first complains of the illogical and unjust discrimination against the Christians and of the calumnies they suffer, and then meets the charge of atheism (a major complaint directed at the Christians of the day was that by disbelieving in the Roman gods, they were showing themselves to be atheists). He establishes the principle of monotheism, citing pagan poets and philosophers in support of the very doctrines for which Christians are condemned, and argues for the superiority of the

Christian belief in God to that of pagans. This first strongly-reasoned argument for the unity of God in Christian literature is supplemented by an able exposition of the Trinity. Assuming then the defensive, he justifies the Christian abstention from worship of the national deities by arguing that it is absurd and indecent, quoting at length the pagan poets and philosophers in support of his contention. Finally, he meets the charges of immorality by exposing the Christian ideal of purity, even in thought, and the inviolable sanctity of the marriage bond. In refuting the charge of cannibalism Athenagoras states that Christians detest all cruelty and murder, refusing to attend contests of gladiators and wild beasts and holding that women who use drugs to bring on abortion commit murder for which they will have to give an account to God.[178]

The treatise on the Resurrection of the Dead, the first complete exposition of the doctrine in Christian literature, was written later than the Apology, to which it may be considered as an appendix. The writer brings to the defense of the doctrine the best that contemporary philosophy could adduce. After meeting the objections common to his time, he seeks to prove the possibility of a resurrection in view either of the power of the Creator, or of the nature of our bodies. To exercise such powers is neither unworthy of God nor unjust to other creatures. He argues that the nature and end of man demand a perpetuation of the life of body and soul. There are reasons to think that De resurrectione is not by Athenagoras but by some 4th-century author, e.g. the use

---

[178] Ante-Nicene Fathers, Vol. II — Writings of Athenagoras — A Plea For the Christians — Chapter XXXV – The Christians Condemn and Detest all Cruelty

of at least one term coined by Philo of Alexandria and not widely known before the time of Origen.

CHAPTER 10 Clement of Alexandria - Christian Theologian

Joel Furches

Quintus Septimius Florens Tertullianus (160 C.E.-225 C.E.) was the first significant Christian author to write in Latin, and one of the most prolific. As early church historian Jerome wrote:

> Now finally Tertullian the presbyter is ranked first of the Latin writers after Victor and Apollonius.

A brilliant writer, he was known for his wit, his biting criticism of opposing viewpoints, and his sarcasm; aspects of his writing that transcend translation such that they are obvious even to the modern English reader. Jerome summed it up well when he said:

> He possessed a sharp and violent talent, and flourished in the reigns of Severus and Caracalla. He wrote many volumes, which I shall omit because they are well-known. I myself saw a certain Paul, an old man of Concordia (which is a town in Italy): he told me that as a youth he had seen a man at Rome, who had been the secretary of the aged Cyprian, and who recalled that Cyprian would never let a day pass without reading Tertullian, and that he often said to him 'Give me my master', clearly meaning Tertullian.

Tertullian did the Church the service of crystalizing the concept of the Trinity (or at least the vocabulary used to describe the Trinity), elucidating the sin nature of man and the salvation purchased by Christ, defending the chain of custody as concerns the truth about Christ, and arguing for the literal second coming of Christ.

Like any human author, Tertullian was not without error. Some of his writings and formulations were later adapted to justify legalistic doctrines such as those advanced by the Roman Catholic Church. But a circumspect examination of his writings is well worth the while of a dedicated student of the history of theology and the Church.

Early Life and Ministry

What information is available on the life and background of Tertullian is either gleaned from clues and scant personal references in his writings, or from church tradition. As a consequence, most of his biography is speculative.

According to Jerome's *De virus illustribus*, Tertullian was the son of a Roman centurion stationed in Carthage in Northern Africa. Tertullian was born and raised in a pagan culture, and clearly received a first-class education in both the Greek and Roman traditions.

It is speculated that Tertullian practiced Law as his profession, mostly because of his heavy use of legal terms and reasoning in his writings. Tertullian's conversion to Christianity occurred well into his adulthood, probably in his 30's or 40's. Much like the Apostle Paul, once Tertullian was converted he launched almost immediately into a zealous defense of the Christian faith, using his extensive education and brilliant intelligence as his weapon. In Carthage where Tertullian lived, the Roman persecution of Christians was extreme. This did not hold Tertullian back from risking his life by directing a number of his writings to the pagan culture, defending the Christian belief and denouncing the pointless torment, they received. Especially representative of this kind of writing is his *Apologeticus*, a book wherein he uses his extensive knowledge of the law to show the injustice of the way in which Christians were being treated and the virtue of Christianity versus the depravity of paganism.

As Tertullian proved himself entirely devoted to the Christian cause, he was soon appointed as an elder in the church at Carthage.

A passionate man, Tertullian was frustrated at the complacency he saw creeping into the church doctrine and leadership. It was perhaps for this reason that later in his ministry, he became enamored of a new sect called Montanism, which was heavily charismatic. Much of his later work was written defending this belief.

Historical Setting

In the second century, Latin as the common language was rapidly replacing Greek. With Rome dominating the world scene for almost 200 years, Hellenistic beliefs and culture were giving way to the Latin mindset, which was more utilitarian and less philosophical.

During this time period, Carthage was a center of heavy persecution for Christians. This extreme persecution had an impact on the doctrine of the church in Carthage and of Tertullian specifically. The persecution was taken as a sign that the return of Christ was imminent, and the church in Carthage proudly embraced persecution and martyrdom as evidences to their commitment to and favor from God. The Church in Carthage tended to look down on those Christians who fled persecution and caved to cultural pressure to hide or denounce their Christian beliefs. Often these people were refused re-entry into the church. Tertullian's beliefs about how Christians were to live and to behave were based on the idea that Christ was going to return at any moment. An example of this was his belief regarding abstinence, which he thought should be practiced universally by both the married and the unmarried. In part because of the rejection of carnal desires in favor of spiritual ones, and in part because he did not think it wise to bring children into the world when Christ would be returning at any moment.

Writings

Tertullian wrote close to fifty known books, thirty-one of which are still extant. The majority of his works were written in response to heresy or a defense of Christianity. Since he never authored a (known) systematic theology, and because his views on some doctrines seemed to fluctuate across his writings, it would be difficult to reconstruct his theology in its entirety.

Tertullian was fluent in both Latin and Greek, and wrote works in both, but the majority of his writings were composed in Latin. While he was never sainted by the Catholic Church, the fact that he wrote in Latin and some of his more legalistic doctrines have made him a favorite of Roman Catholics. He was influential in their ideas on baptism and on the virtues of life-long abstinence.

Tertullian's writings were largely reactive in nature. He wrote to address challenges to his beliefs from within and without the Christian Church. He wrote to the surrounding culture, denouncing the reasonless attacks they made on Christians and condemning their hedonistic and bloodthirsty ways in his brilliant *Apologeticus*. He wrote against a variety of doctrines, especially those that used Aristotelian philosophy to support "Christian" beliefs. He is famous for having said "What has Athens to do with Jerusalem?" meaning that one should lean on what the Apostles received from Christ and not Hellenistic ideas in order to support the Church's doctrine:

> All doctrine which agrees with the apostolic churches, those nurseries and original depositories of faith, must be regarded as truth, and as undoubtedly constituting what the churches received from the Apostles, what the Apostles received from Christ, and what Christ received from God.

-Prescription against Heretics 21

Teachings

Tertullian was the type of person who had an opinion on practically everything. Volumes could be written on the things he strongly believed and on how his beliefs changed over time. Because Tertullian strongly disliked Platonist philosophy, he tended toward an extreme materialism. He believed, for instance, that the Spirit, which people received at baptism, was a material substance that mixed with the water and physically entered the body of the believer.

Tertullian was also fairly legalistic in some of his views. He considered the New Testament injunctions to physical purity to be transitionary, meaning that they did not go far enough. Since (he said) Jesus and Paul were introducing a new belief system to sinful pagans, they commanded behaviors that were achievable by those people. As time goes on, however, Christians needed to act in ways that were more and more austere and becoming to their belief system. So whereas Christ commanded no divorce except in the case of infidelity, Tertullian suggested that Christians take the next step, so to speak, and never divorce for any reason. Whereas Paul condemned sexual activity except in the case of marriage, Tertullian said that the next obvious stage was no sexual activity whatsoever. While he believed that baptism removed a person's sins, he was against infant baptism because he believed the person should make a conscious decision to have their sins removed. He suggested people wait until well into their adulthood to be baptized, as the removal of sin was a one-time occurrence, and they should be at a point in their life where they were not liable to sin anymore.

These are, of course, examples of Tertullian's more extreme positions. Much of what he wrote has informed theology and doctrine up to present time.

One of Tertullian's biggest contributions to theology is what he wrote on the Trinity. Believers had long recognized the distinction between the Father, the Son, and the Holy Spirit, but there was still a struggle theologically to reconcile the three. Three concepts that some early theologians advanced to explain the distinction between the Father and the Son were Subordinationism, Adoptionism and Modalism. Subordinationism taught that the Son was divine but inferior and subordinate to the Father. Adoptionists taught that Christ was a natural human being that was overcome or infused by God with divinity. This preserved monotheism at the expense of the deity of Christ. Modalism said that The Father, the Son, and the Holy Spirit were simply roles that God adopted at any particular time, or "masks" that God wore, similar to an actor taking on a character in a play. In his book *Our Legacy*, Dr. John Hannah says:

> Though the early church leaders rejected Adoptionism and Modalism as well as set forth arguments for the deity of Christ, they were not able to articulate the Trinity of God without appearing to express the distinction between the Father and the Son in some form of Subordinationism ... more than any other early church leader (Tertullian) developed the distinct terminology for the discussion of the doctrine of God.

-John Hannah, *Our Legacy*, page 78

Tertullian coined the words "Trinity" (*trinitas*), "Persons" (*persona*), and "Substance" (*essential/ substantia*) in reference to the triune nature of God, terms that have been adopted into the creedal phrase "Three persons, one substance" that is still used in most mainstream denominations.

> Everywhere I hold one substance in three cohering... All are of one, by unity of substance; while the mystery of the dispensation is still guarded, which distributes the Unity into Trinity, placing in their order the three, the Father, the Son, and the Holy Spirit; three however... not in substance but in form, not in power but in appearance.

122

-Tertullian, *Against Praxeas*

Another important contribution Tertullian made to the doctrine of the early church was his assertion regarding the sin nature of humans, and the necessary sacrifice of Christ. Dr. Hannah explains Tertullian's writings on sin nature:

> Tertullian... viewed Adam as a historical figure and the human soul as having been created by God in him and passed, along with the body, from parent to child (a view called traducianism). "We acknowledge, therefore, that life begins with conception, because we contend that the soul begins at conception. Life begins with the soul begins." (*The Soul* 27). Further, he argued that every soul, though possessed of free will, is innately stained with the result of Adam's error. However, he did not set forth a clear doctrine of Adamic solidarity by explaining the manner of our participation in Adam's progeny. Instead, our inheritance from Adam is a disordered sensuality, a proneness to irrationality. In the matter of inability and freedom, Tertullian was inconsistent. He waffled between the two views, first asserting one and then the other without seeking to explain how both might be valid. "Some things are by virtue of the divine compassion, and some things are by virtue of our agency" (21). However, he stated that as the branch of a wicked tree cannot bear good fruit unless it be grafted into a good tree, and as the branches are not self-grafting agents, so God's grace is greater than our free wills.

-John Hanna, *Our Legacy*, pages 208-209

And his view on Christ's sacrifice:

> (Tertullian) carried his training in law into the defense of Christianity. Understanding that an offense mandated a recompense, he argued that Christ lived and died for the sinner, satisfying God for wrongs done. In doing so he became the first church leader to use the term "satisfaction" in reference to our Lord's death.

> -John Hanna, *Our Legacy*, page 153

As mentioned previously, the imminent return of Christ was a very heavy influence in Tertullian's beliefs and ways of thinking. Since Christianity had been around for almost 200 years by this time, many Christians were becoming disillusioned over the fact that Christ had not yet returned. Some Christian leaders were beginning to teach that the return of Christ was spiritual and allegorical. Tertullian defended end-times prophecy as a literal return of Christ:

> We confess that a kingdom has been promised to us on earth, but before heaven and in another state of existence. It will be after the resurrection for a thousand years in the divinely built city of Jerusalem, let down from heaven... After its thousand years are over, during which period the resurrection of the saints will be completed, who will rise earlier or later according to their merits, there will be the destruction of the world and the conflagration at the judgment.

> -*Against Marcion* 3.24.3

Conclusion

In the online database, "Theopedia," the entry on Tertullian has this to say:

> Tertullian's *Apology (Apologeticus)* is one of the best-known works of the pre-Nicene era. In it, he provides not only a stirring defense of Christianity to the Roman rulers, but takes exhaustive measures to show that Roman culture and religion is inferior and hopeless when compared to Christianity.

This ancient work is surprisingly appropriate for a modern audience in an age and culture, which is rapidly adopting the mindset and values of pagan cultures, and increasingly condemning and criminalizing Christianity while promoting practically every other belief system. The modern Christian would do well to study the writings of a man so well acquainted with cultural persecution. Tertullian's work is also worth studying for a window into the thought that has shaped modern theology on both sides of the fence. He was a man of great intellect and passion and a worthy addition to any Christian's library.

CHAPTER 11 Cyprian of Carthage

CHAPTER 11

Cyprian (Latin: Thascius Caecilius Cyprianus) (c. 200 – September 14, 258 C.E.)[179] was bishop of Carthage and an important Early Christian writer, many of whose Latin works are extant. He was born around the beginning of the 3rd century in North Africa, perhaps at Carthage, where he received a classical education. After converting to Christianity, he became a bishop in 249 and eventually died a martyr at Carthage.

Early Life

Cyprian was born sometime in the early third century. He was a leading member of legal fraternity in Carthage, He was well into middle age when he was converted to Christianity and baptised. The site of his eventual martyrdom was his own villa. Before becoming a Christian, he was an orator, "pleader in the courts", and a teacher of rhetoric. The date of his conversion is unknown, but after his baptism about 245–248 he gave away a portion of his wealth to the poor of Carthage, as befitted a man of his status.

His original name was Thascius; he took the additional name Caecilius in memory of the presbyter to whom he owed his conversion. In the early days of his conversion he wrote an Epistola ad Donatum de gratia Dei and the Testimoniorum Libri III that adhere closely to

---

[179] http://en.wikipedia.org/wiki/Cyprian_of_Carthage

the models of Tertullian, who influenced his style and thinking.

His Contested Election as Bishop of Carthage

Not long after his baptism he was ordained deacon, and soon afterward presbyter; and sometime between July 248 and April 249 he was chosen bishop of Carthage, a popular choice among the poor who remembered his patronage as demonstrating good equestrian style, while a portion of the presbytery opposed it, for all Cyprian's wealth and learning and diplomacy and literary talents. Moreover, the opposition within the church community at Carthage did not dissolve during his episcopacy.

Soon, however, the entire community was put to an unwanted test. Christians in North Africa had not suffered persecution for many years; the church was assured and lax. Early in 250 the "Decian persecution" began. Measures were first taken demanding that the bishops and officers of the church sacrifice to the emperor. The proconsul on circuit, and five commissioners for each town, administered the edict; but, when the proconsul reached Carthage, Cyprian had fled.

It is quite evident in the writings of the church fathers from various dioceses that the Christian community was divided on this occasion, among those who stood firm in civil disobedience, and those who buckled, submitting in word or in deed to the order of sacrifice and receiving a ticket or receipt called a "libellus." Cyprian's secret departure from Carthage was interpreted by his enemies as cowardice and infidelity, and they hastened to accuse him at Rome. The Roman clergy wrote to Cyprian in terms of disapproval. Cyprian rejoined that he fled in accordance with visions and the divine command. From his place of refuge, he ruled his flock with earnestness and zeal, using a faithful deacon as his intermediary.

Controversy over the Lapsed

The persecution was especially severe at Carthage, according to Church sources. Many Christians fell away, and were thereafter referred to as "lapsi", but afterwards asked to be received again into the Church. Their requests were granted early, with no regard being paid to the demand of Cyprian and his faithful among the Carthaginian clergy, who insisted upon earnest repentance. The confessors among the more liberal group intervened to allow hundreds of the lapsed to return to the Church.

Though he had remained in seclusion himself, Cyprian now censured all laxity toward the lapsed, refused absolution to them except in case of mortal sickness, and desired to postpone the question of their re-admission to the Church to quieter times. A schism broke out in Carthage. Felicissimus, who had been ordained deacon by the presbyter Novatus during the absence of Cyprian, opposed all steps taken by Cyprian's representatives. Cyprian deposed and excommunicated him and his supporter Augendius. Felicissimus was upheld by Novatus and four other presbyters, and a determined opposition was thus organized.

When, after an absence of fourteen months, Cyprian returned to his diocese, he defended leaving his post in letters to the other North African bishops and a tract "De lapsis," and called a council of North African bishops at

Carthage to consider the treatment of the lapsed and the apparent schism of Felicissimus (251). The council in the main sided with Cyprian and condemned Felicissimus, though no acts of this council survive. The "libellatici" were to be restored at once upon sincere repentance; but such as had taken part in heathen sacrifices could be received back into the Church only when on the point of death. Afterward this regulation was essentially mitigated, and even these were restored if they repented immediately after a sudden fall and eagerly sought absolution; though clerics who had fallen were to be deposed and could not be restored to their functions.

In Carthage the followers of Felicissimus elected Fortunatus as bishop in opposition to Cyprian, while in Rome the followers of the Roman presbyter Novatian, who also refused absolution to all the lapsed, elected their man as bishop of Rome, in opposition to Cornelius. The Novatianists secured the election of a rival bishop of their own at Carthage, Maximus by name. Novatus now left Felicissimus and followed the Novatian party.

But these extremes strengthened the firm but moderating influence exhibited in Cyprian's writings, and the following of his opponents grew less and less. He rose still higher in the favor of the people when they witnessed his self-denying devotion during the time of a great plague and famine.

He comforted his brethren by writing his "De mortalitate," and in his "De eleemosynis" exhorted them to active charity towards the poor, while he set the best pattern by his own life. He defended Christianity and the Christians in the apologia "Ad Demetrianum," directed against a certain Demetrius and the reproach of the heathens that Christians were the cause of the public calamities.

Persecution under Valerian[edit]

At the end of 256 a new persecution of the Christians under Emperor Valerian I broke out, and both Pope Stephen I and his successor, Pope Sixtus II, suffered martyrdom at Rome.

In Africa Cyprian courageously prepared his people for the expected edict of persecution by his "De exhortatione martyrii," and himself set an example when he was brought before the Roman proconsul Aspasius Paternus (August 30, 257). He refused to sacrifice to the pagan deities and firmly professed Christ.

The consul banished him to Curubis, modern Korba, whence he comforted to the best of his ability his flock and his banished clergy. In a vision he saw his approaching fate. When a year had passed he was recalled and kept practically a prisoner in his own villa, in expectation of severer measures after a new and more stringent imperial edict arrived, demanding the execution of all Christian clerics, according to reports of it by Christian writers.

On September 13, 258, he was imprisoned at the behest of the new proconsul, Galerius Maximus. The day following he was examined for the last time and sentenced to die by the sword. His only answer was "Thanks be to God!" The execution was carried out at once in an open place near the city. A vast multitude followed Cyprian on his last journey. He removed his garments without assistance, knelt down, and prayed. After he blindfolded himself, he was beheaded by the sword.

The body was interred by Christian hands near the place of execution, and over it, as well as on the actual scene of his death, churches were afterward erected, which, however, were destroyed by the Vandals. Charlemagne is said to have had the bones transferred to France, and Lyons, Arles, Venice, Compiegne, and Roenay in Flanders claim the possession of the martyr's relics.

Writings

Wikisource has original works written by or about Cyprian[180]

Cyprian's works were edited in volumes 3 and 4 of the Patrologia Latina. Besides a number of epistles, which are partly collected with the answers of those to whom they were written, Cyprian wrote a number of treatises, some of which have also the character of pastoral letters.

His most important work is his "De unitate ecclesiae." In it, he states: "He can no longer have God for his Father who has not the Church for his mother; . . . he who gathereth elsewhere than in the Church scatters the Church of Christ" (vi.); "nor is there any other home to believers but the one Church" (ix.).

The following works are of doubtful authenticity: De spectaculis ("On Public Games"); De bono pudicitiae ("The Virtue of Modesty"); De idolorum vanitate ("On the Vanity of Images," written by Novatian); De laude martyrii ("In Praise of Martyrs"); Adversus aleatores; De duobus montibus Sina et Sion (On the Two Mountains Sinai and Zion); Adversus Judaeos; and the Cena Cypriani ("Cyprian's Banquet", which enjoyed wide circulation in the Middle Ages). The treatise entitled De duplici

---

[180] http://en.wikisource.org/wiki/Author:Cyprian

martyrio ad Fortunatum and attributed to Cyprian was not only published by Erasmus, but probably also composed by him.

The Plague of Cyprian is named after him due to his description of it.

St Cyprian's first writing starts out as a speech he made to his friends. It is called, Ad Donatum. It speaks out against the Roman Government and gladiator shows. He says that the only refuge from these evils is the prayerful life of a Christian. St. Cyprian was the first great Latin writer among the Christians. Until the days of Jerome and Augustine, Cyprian's writings had no rivals in the West.

CHAPTER 12 Tertullian - Defense of Christianity

Joel Furches

Quintus Septimius Florens Tertullianus (160 C.E. 225 C.E.) was the first significant Christian author to write in Latin, and one of the most prolific. As early church historian Jerome wrote:

> Now finally Tertullian the presbyter is ranked first of the Latin writers after Victor and Apollonius.

A brilliant writer, he was known for his wit, his biting criticism of opposing viewpoints, and his sarcasm; aspects of his writing that transcend translation such that they are obvious even to the modern English reader. Jerome summed it up well when he said:

> He possessed a sharp and violent talent, and flourished in the reigns of Severus and Caracalla. He wrote many volumes, which I shall omit because they are well-known. I myself saw a certain Paul, an old man of Concordia (which is a town in Italy): he told me that as a youth he had seen a man at Rome, who had been the secretary of the aged Cyprian, and who recalled that Cyprian would never let a day pass without reading Tertullian, and that he often said to him 'Give me my master', clearly meaning Tertullian.

Tertullian did the Church the service of crystalizing the concept of the Trinity (or at least the vocabulary used to describe the Trinity), elucidating the sin nature of man and the salvation purchased by Christ, defending the chain of custody as concerns the truth about Christ, and arguing for the literal second coming of Christ.

Like any human author, Tertullian was not without error. Some of his writings and formulations were later adapted to justify legalistic doctrines such as those advanced by the Roman Catholic Church. However, a circumspect examination of his writings is well worth the while of a dedicated student of the history of theology and the Church.

Early Life and Ministry

What information is available on the life and background of Tertullian is gleaned either from clues and scant personal references in his writings, or from church tradition. Consequently, most of his biography is speculative.

According to Jerome's *De virus illustribus*, Tertullian was the son of a Roman centurion stationed in Carthage in Northern Africa. Tertullian was born and raised in a pagan culture, and clearly received a first-class education in both the Greek and Roman traditions.

It is speculated that Tertullian practiced Law as his profession, mostly because of his heavy use of legal terms and reasoning in his writings. Tertullian's conversion to Christianity occurred well into his adulthood, probably in his 30's or 40's.

Much like the Apostle Paul, once Tertullian was converted he launched almost immediately into a zealous defense of the Christian faith, using his extensive education and brilliant intelligence as his weapon. In

Carthage where Tertullian lived, the Roman persecution of Christians was extreme. This did not hold Tertullian back from risking his life by directing a number of his writings to the pagan culture, defending the Christian belief and denouncing the pointless torment they received. Especially representative of this kind of writing is his *Apologeticus*, a book wherein he uses his extensive knowledge of the law to show the injustice of the way in which Christians were being treated and the virtue of Christianity versus the depravity of paganism.

As Tertullian proved himself entirely devoted to the Christian cause, he was soon appointed as an elder in the church at Carthage.

A passionate man, Tertullian was frustrated at the complacency he saw creeping into the church doctrine and leadership. It was perhaps for this reason that later in his ministry, he became enamored of a new sect called Montanism, which was heavily charismatic. Much of his later work was written defending this belief.

Historical Setting

In the second century, Latin as the common language was rapidly replacing Greek. With Rome dominating the world scene for almost 200 years, Hellenistic beliefs and culture were giving way to the Latin mindset, which was more utilitarian and less philosophical.

During this time period, Carthage was a center of heavy persecution for Christians. This extreme persecution had an impact on the doctrine of the church in Carthage and of Tertullian specifically. The persecution was taken as a sign that the return of Christ was imminent, and the church in Carthage proudly embraced persecution and martyrdom as evidences to their commitment to and favor from God. The Church in Carthage tended to look down on those Christians who fled persecution and caved to cultural pressure to hide or denounce their Christian beliefs. Often these people were refused re-entry into the church. Tertullian's beliefs about how Christians were to live and to behave were based on the idea that Christ was going to return at any moment. An example of this was his belief regarding abstinence, which he thought should be practiced universally by both the married and the unmarried; in part because of the rejection of carnal desires in favor of spiritual ones, and in part because he did not think it wise to bring children into the world when Christ would be returning at any moment.

Writings

Tertullian wrote close to fifty known books, thirty-one of which are still extant. The majority of his works were written in response to heresy or a defense of Christianity. Since he never authored a (known) systematic theology, and because his views on some doctrines seemed to fluctuate across his writings, it would be difficult to reconstruct his theology in its entirety.

Tertullian was fluent in both Latin and Greek, and wrote works in both, but the majority of his writings were composed in Latin. While he was never sainted by the Catholic Church, the fact that he wrote in Latin and some of his more legalistic doctrines have made him a favorite of Roman Catholics. He was influential in their ideas on baptism and on the virtues of life-long abstinence.

Tertullian's writings were largely reactive in nature. He wrote to address challenges to his beliefs from within and without the Christian Church. He wrote to the surrounding culture, denouncing the reasonless attacks they made on Christians and condemning their hedonistic and bloodthirsty ways in his brilliant *Apologeticus*. He wrote against a variety of doctrines, especially those that used Aristotelian philosophy to support "Christian" beliefs. He is famous for having said "What has Athens to do with Jerusalem?" meaning that one should lean on what the Apostles received from Christ and not Hellenistic ideas in order to support the Church's doctrine:

> All doctrine which agrees with the apostolic churches, those nurseries and original depositories of faith, must be regarded as truth, and as undoubtedly constituting what the churches received from the Apostles, what the Apostles received from Christ, and what Christ received from God.

> -*Prescription against Heretics* 21

Teachings

Tertullian was the type of person who had an opinion on practically everything. Volumes could be written on the things he strongly believed and on how his beliefs changed over time. Because Tertullian strongly disliked Platonist philosophy, he tended toward an extreme materialism. He believed, for instance, that the Spirit which people received at baptism was a material substance that mixed with the water and physically entered the body of the believer.

Tertullian was also fairly legalistic in some of his views. He considered the New Testament injunctions to physical purity to be transitionary, meaning that they did not go far enough. Since (he said) Jesus and Paul were introducing a new belief system to sinful pagans, they commanded behaviors that were achievable by those people. As time goes on, however, Christians needed to act in ways that were more and more austere and becoming to their belief system. So whereas Christ commanded no divorce except in the case of infidelity, Tertullian suggested that Christians take the next step, so to speak, and never divorce for any reason. Whereas Paul condemned sexual activity except in the case of marriage, Tertullian said that the next obvious stage was no sexual activity whatsoever. While he believed that baptism removed a person's sins, he was against infant baptism because he believed the person should make a conscious decision to have their sins removed. He suggested people wait until well into their adulthood to be baptized, as the removal of sin was a one-time occurrence, and they should be at a point in their life where they were not liable to sin anymore.

These are, of course, examples of Tertullian's more extreme positions. Much of what he wrote has informed theology and doctrine up to present time.

One of Tertullian's most important contributions to theology is what he wrote on the Trinity. The distinction between the Father, the Son, and the Holy Spirit had long been recognized by believers, but there was still a struggle theologically to reconcile the three. Three concepts that some early theologians advanced to explain the distinction between the Father and the Son were Subordinationism, Adoptionism and Modalism. Subordinationism taught that the Son was divine but inferior and subordinate to the Father. Adoptionists taught that Christ was a natural human being that was overcome or infused by God with divinity. This preserved monotheism at the expense of the deity of Christ. Modalism said that The Father, the Son, and the Holy Spirit were simply roles that God adopted at any particular time, or "masks" that God wore, similar to an actor taking on a character in a play. In his book *Our Legacy*, Dr. John Hannah says:

> Though the early church leaders rejected Adoptionism and Modalism as well as set forth arguments for the deity of Christ, they were not able to articulate the Trinity of God without appearing to express the distinction between the Father and the Son in some form of Subordinationism ... more than any other early church leader (Tertullian) developed the distinct terminology for the discussion of the doctrine of God.

-John Hannah, Our Legacy, page 78

Tertullian coined the words "Trinity" (*trinitas*), "Persons" (*persona*), and "Substance" (*essential/ substantia*) in reference to the triune nature of God, terms that have been adopted into the creedal phrase "Three persons, one substance" that is still used in most mainstream denominations.

> Everywhere I hold one substance in three cohering... All are of one, by unity of substance; while the mystery of the dispensation is still guarded, which distributes the Unity into Trinity, placing in their order the three, the Father, the Son, and the Holy Spirit;

three however... not in substance but in form,
not in power but in appearance.

-Tertullian, *Against Praxeas*

Another important contribution Tertullian made to
the doctrine of the early church was his assertion
regarding the sin nature of humans, and the necessary
sacrifice of Christ. Dr. Hannah explains Tertullian's
writings on sin nature:

Tertullian... viewed Adam as a historical
figure and the human soul as having been
created by God in him and passed, along with
the body, from parent to child (a view called
traducianism). "We acknowledge, therefore,
that life begins with conception, because we
contend that the soul begins at conception. Life
begins with the soul begins." (*The Soul* 27).
Further, he argued that every soul, though
possessed of free will, is innately stained with
the result of Adam's error. However, he did
not set forth a clear doctrine of Adamic
solidarity by explaining the manner of our
participation in Adam's progeny. Instead, our
inheritance from Adam is a disordered
sensuality, a proneness to irrationality. In the
matter of inability and freedom, Tertullian was
inconsistent. He waffled between the two
views, first asserting one and then the other
without seeking to explain how both might be
valid. "Some things are by virtue of the divine
compassion, and some things are by virtue of
our agency" (21). However, he stated that as
the branch of a wicked tree cannot bear good
fruit unless it be grafted into a good tree, and

as the branches are not self-grafting agents, so God's grace is greater than our free wills.

-John Hanna, *Our Legacy*, pages 208-209

And his view on Christ's sacrifice:

(Tertullian) carried his training in law into the defense of Christianity. Understanding that an offense mandated a recompense, he argued that Christ lived and died for the sinner, satisfying God for wrongs done. In doing so he became the first church leader to use the term "satisfaction" in reference to our Lord's death.

-John Hanna, *Our Legacy*, page 153

As mentioned previously, the imminent return of Christ was a very heavy influence in Tertullian's beliefs and ways of thinking. Since Christianity had been around for almost 200 years by this time, many Christians were becoming disillusioned over the fact that Christ had not yet returned. Some Christian leaders were beginning to teach that the return of Christ was spiritual and allegorical. Tertullian defended end-times prophecy as a literal return of Christ:

We confess that a kingdom has been promised to us on earth, but before heaven and in another state of existence. It will be after the resurrection for a thousand years in the divinely built city of Jerusalem, let down from heaven... After its thousand years are over, during which period the resurrection of the saints will be completed, who will rise earlier or later according to their merits, there will be the destruction of the world and the conflagration at the judgment.

-Against Marcion 3.24.3

Conclusion

In the online database, "Theopedia," the entry on Tertullian has this to say:

> Tertullian's *Apology (Apologeticus)* is one of the best-known works of the pre-Nicene era. In it, he provides not only a stirring defense of Christianity to the Roman rulers, but takes exhaustive measures to show that Roman culture and religion is inferior and hopeless when compared to Christianity.

This ancient work is surprisingly appropriate for a modern audience in an age and culture which is rapidly adopting the mindset and values of pagan cultures, and increasingly condemning and criminalizing Christianity while promoting practically every other belief system. The modern Christian would do well to study the writings of a man so well-acquainted with cultural persecution. Tertullian's work is also worth studying for a window into the thought that has shaped modern theology on both sides of the fence. He was a man of great intellect and passion and a worthy addition to any Christian's library.

CHAPTER 13 Hippolytus of Rome

Hippolytus of Rome (170–235 C.E.)[181] was the most important 3rd-century theologian in the Christian Church in Rome, where he was probably born. Photios I of Constantinople describes him in his Bibliotheca (cod. 121) as a disciple of Irenaeus, who was said to be a disciple of Polycarp, and from the context of this passage it is supposed that he suggested that Hippolytus himself so styled himself. However, this assertion is doubtful. He came into conflict with the popes of his time and seems to have headed a schismatic group as a rival bishop of Rome.[2] For that reason he is sometimes considered the first antipope. He opposed the Roman bishops who softened the penitential system to accommodate the large number of new pagan converts. However, he was very probably reconciled to the Church when he died as a martyr.

Starting in the 4th century, various legends arose about him, identifying him as a priest of the Novatianist schism or as a soldier converted by Saint Laurence. He has also been confused with another martyr of the same name.

Life and Ministry

As a presbyter of the church at Rome under Pope Zephyrinus (199–217), Hippolytus was distinguished for

---

[181] http://en.wikipedia.org/wiki/Hippolytus_of_Rome

his learning and eloquence. It was at this time that Origen of Alexandria, then a young man, heard him preach.[4]

He accused Pope Zephyrinus of modalism, the heresy which held that the names Father and Son are simply different names for the same subject.[5] Hippolytus championed the Logos doctrine of the Greek apologists, most notably Justin Martyr, which distinguished the Father from the Logos ("Word"). An ethical conservative, he was scandalized when Pope Callixtus I (217–222) extended absolution to Christians who had committed grave sins, such as adultery.[182] At this time, he seems to have allowed himself to be elected as a rival Bishop of Rome, and continued to attack Pope Urban I (222–230) and Pope Pontian (230–235).

Under the persecution by Emperor Maximinus Thrax, Hippolytus and Pontian were exiled together in 235 to Sardinia, and it is very probably that, before his death there, he was reconciled to the other party at Rome, for, under Pope Fabian (236–250), his body and that of Pontian were brought to Rome. From the so-called chronography of the year 354 (more precisely, the Catalogus Liberianus, or Liberian Catalogue) we learn that on August 13, probably in 236, the two bodies were interred in Rome, that of Hippolytus in a cemetery on the Via Tiburtina, his funeral being conducted by Justin the Confessor. This document indicates that, by about 255, Hippolytus was considered a martyr and gives him the rank of a priest, not of a bishop, an indication that before his death the schismatic was received again into the bosom of the Church, or that significant action was

---

[182] Saint Hippolytus of Rome." Encyclopædia Britannica. 2010. Encyclopædia Britannica Online. 15 Aug. 2010

taken at least posthumously to ensure no lasting schism between both popes' followers.[citation needed]

Legends

The facts of his life as well as his writing were soon forgotten in the West, perhaps by reason of his schismatic activities and because he wrote in Greek. Pope Damasus I dedicated to him one of his famous epigrams, making him, however, a priest of the Novatianist schism, a view later accepted by Prudentius in the 5th century in his "Passion of St Hippolytus". In the Passionals of the 7th and 8th centuries he is represented as a soldier converted by Saint Lawrence, a legend that long survived in the Roman Breviary. He was also confused with a martyr of the same name who was buried in Portus, of which city he was believed to have been a bishop. Prudentius seems to have drawn on the story of the mythological Hippolytus for his description of the death of the saint, picturing him as dragged to death by wild horses at Ostia. He described the subterranean tomb of the saint and states that he saw there a picture representing Hippolytus' execution. He also confirms August 13 as the date on which Hippolytus was celebrated.

This account led to Hippolytus being considered the patron saint of horses. During the Middle Ages, sick horses were brought to St Ippolyts, Hertfordshire, England, where a church is dedicated to him.[183]

---

[183] Ippollitts (A Guide to Old Hertfordshire)

Writings

In 1551 a marble statue of a seated figure (originally female, perhaps personifying one of the sciences) was found in the cemetery of the Via Tiburtina and was heavily restored. On the sides of the seat was carved a paschal cycle, and on the back the titles of numerous writings by Hippolytus. Many other works are listed by Eusebius of Caesarea and Jerome.

Hippolytus's principal work is the Refutation of all Heresies. Of its ten books, Book I was the most important.[184] It was long known and was printed (with the title Philosophumena) among the works of Origen. Books II and III are lost, and Books IV–X were found, without the name of the author, in a monastery of Mount Athos in 1842. E. Miller published them in 1851 under the title Philosophumena, attributing them to Origen of Alexandria. They have since been attributed to Hippolytus.

Hippolytus's voluminous writings, which for variety of subject can be compared with those of Origen of Alexandria, embrace the spheres of exegesis, homiletics, apologetics and polemic, chronography, and ecclesiastical law. Hippolytus recorded the first liturgical reference to the Virgin Mary, as part of the ordination rite of a bishop.[185]

His works have unfortunately come down to us in such a fragmentary condition that it is difficult to obtain

---

[184] Saint Hippolytus of Rome." Encyclopædia Britannica. 2010. Encyclopædia Britannica Online. 15 Aug. 2010

[185] McNally, Terrence, What Every Catholic Should Know about Mary 2009

from them any very exact notion of his intellectual and literary importance.

Of exegetical works usually attributed to Hippolytus, the best preserved are the Commentary on the Prophet Daniel and the Commentary on the Song of Songs. This is the earliest attested Christian interpretation of the Song, covering only the first three chapters to Song 3:7. Hippolytus' Commentary on the Song of Songs interprets the Song as referring to a complicated relationship between Israel, Christ and the Gentile Church. Christ as the Logos is represented in various richly symbolic ways: as the Feminine Sophia ("Wisdom"), who was God's agent in creation and later lived with Solomon and inspired the prophets, as the transgendered maker of wine (like Dionysus) that nurtures the Church with his breasts (the Law and the Gospel), as the victorious Helios who rides across the sky and gathers the nations. The commentary returns often to the topic of the anointing of the Holy Spirit and was originally written as a mystagogy, an instruction for new Christians. Scholars have usually assumed the Commentary On the Song of Songs was originally composed for use during Passover, a season favored in the West for Baptisms (see Hippolytus' Commentary on Daniel 1.17). The commentary on the Song of Songs survives in two Georgian manuscripts, a Greek epitome, a Paleo-Slavonic florilegium, and fragments in Armenian and Syriac as well as in many patristic quotations, especially in Ambrose of Milan's Exposition on Psalm 118 (119). Hippolytus differed from Origen, who interpreted the Song largely as an allegory of the soul and Christ. Hippolytus, on the other hand, interpreted the Song as a typological treatment of the relationship between the Church of the Circumcision typified by Israel and replaced by the Church composed of both believing Jews and Gentile

Christians. Hippolytus interpreted the Song using the common rhetorical device of ekphrasis, a method of persuasion employed by rhetoricians of the Second Sophistic that used well known themes from popular graphic representations common on household walls as murals and on floors as mosaics. He also supplied his commentary with a fully developed introduction known as the schema isagogicum, indicating his knowledge of the rhetorical conventions for teachers discussing classical works. Origen felt that the Song should be reserved for the spiritually mature and that studying it might be harmful for the novice. In this he followed 3rd-century Jewish interpretive traditions, whereas Hippolytus ignored them.

We are unable to form an opinion of Hippolytus as a preacher, for the Homilies on the Feast of Epiphany which go under his name are wrongly attributed to him.

Of the dogmatic works, On Christ and the Antichrist survives in a complete state. Among other things it includes a vivid account of the events preceding the end of the world, and it was probably written at the time of the persecution under Septimius Severus, about 202.

The influence of Hippolytus was felt chiefly through his works on chronography and ecclesiastical law. His chronicle of the world, a compilation embracing the whole period from the creation of the world up to the year 234, formed a basis for many chronographical works both in the East and West.

In the great compilations of ecclesiastical law that arose in the East since the 4th century, the Church Orders many canons were attributed to Hippolytus, for example in the Canons of Hippolytus or the The Constitutions through Hippolytus. How much of this material is genuinely his, how much of it worked over, and how much of it wrongly attributed to him, can no longer be determined beyond dispute even by the most learned investigation, however a great deal was incorporated into the Fetha Negest, which once served as the constitutional basis of law in Ethiopia — where he is still remembered as Abulides. During the early 20th century the work known as The Egyptian Church Order was identified as the Apostolic Tradition and attributed to Hippolytus; nowaday this attribution is hotly contested.

Differences in style and theology lead some scholars to conclude that some the works attributed to Hippolytus actually derive from a second author.

Two small but potentially important works of Hippolytus, On the Twelve Apostles of Christ, and On the Seventy Apostles of Christ, were often neglected, because the manuscripts were lost during most of the church age and found late, thus people were not sure if they are original or spurious. The two are included in an appendix to the works of Hippolytus in the voluminous collection of Early Church Fathers.

Feast Days

In the Eastern Orthodox Church, the feast day of St Hippolytus falls on August 13, which is also the Apodosis of the Feast of the Transfiguration. Because on the Apodosis the hymns of the Transfiguration are to be repeated, the feast of St. Hippolytus may be transferred to the day before or to some other convenient day. The Eastern Orthodox Church also celebrates the feast of "St Hippolytus Pope of Rome" on January 30, who may or may not be the same individual.

The Roman Catholic Church celebrates St Hippolytus jointly with St Pontian on August 13. The feast of Saint

Hippolytus formerly celebrated on 22 August (see General Roman Calendar as in 1954) was a duplicate of the 13 August feast and for that reason was deleted when the Roman Catholic calendar of saints was revised in 1960. Earlier editions of the Roman Martyrology referred to the 22 August Hippolytus as Bishop of Porto, but the Catholic Encyclopedia sees this as "connected with the confusion regarding the Roman presbyter resulting from the Acts of the Martyrs of Porto. It has not been ascertained whether the memory of the latter was localized at Porto merely in connection with the legend in Prudentius, without further foundation, or whether a person named Hippolytus was really martyred at Porto, and afterwards confounded in legend with Hippolytus of Rome."[12] This opinion is shared by a Benedictine source.[13]

Earlier editions of the Roman Martyrology also mentioned on 30 January a Hippolytus venerated at Antioch, but the details it gave were borrowed from the story of Hippolytus of Rome.[14] Modern editions of the Roman Martyrology omit all mention of this supposed distinct Saint Hippolytus of Antioch.

CHAPTER 14 Theophilus of Antioch - Valuable Testimony

Kyle J. Clark

"[Y]ou call me a Christian, as if this were a damning name to bear, I, for my part, avow that I am a Christian, and bear this name beloved of God, hoping to be serviceable to God." [186]

Antioch was the first location in which followers of Jesus were given the label "Christians," a term meaning "little Christs." Theophilus made it clear in his surviving work, *To Autolycus*, this title was not something to be shunned, but rather to rejoice as if it were a badge of honor. It is through the valuable testimony of Theophilus we learn more about the culture and worldview of the Roman Empire in the second century. It is also through this testimony where we learn of the misunderstandings and rumors that circulated concerning early Christianity.

Theophilus was an apologist, a defender of the Christian faith, in a culture that was often hostile towards believers. However, Theophilus was not only a defender of the Christian worldview, he also attacked the immorality of the religions and mythology of the culture of his time. While he stood in the shadows of great apologists in this time, Theophilus of Antioch undertook the role in persuading others of the truth of Christianity.

Early Life and Ministry

---

[186] (Theophilus 1885, 89)

Theophilus of Antioch was born in approximately 115. Very little is known of his early life, though he admits he was a skeptic and did not embrace Christianity initially. Theophilus related in his one surviving work, *To Autolycus*, that he came to Christianity after studying the writings of the Old Testament. Specifically, he wrote,

> ...I met with the sacred Scriptures of the holy prophets, who also by the Spirit of God foretold the things that have already happened, just as they came to pass, and the things now occurring as they are now happening, and things future in the order in which they shall be accomplished. Admitting, therefore, the proof which events happening as predicted afford, I do not disbelieve, but I believe, obedient to God...[187]

Little is known about his ministry prior to his appointment as Bishop of Antioch. This appointment was made in 168, and he served in this position until dying sometime in the 180s. First century Antioch became a haven to Christians who fled Jerusalem under the persecution of the Jews in the 30s. Antioch was one of the five major Christian centers, the others being Alexandria, Ephesus, Jerusalem, and Rome. Peter is the only documented disciple to have visited Antioch, but we know the Apostle Paul visited there also, and embarked on his missionary journeys here. Growing up in this locale Theophilus would have learned of the martyrdom of the

---

[187] (Theophilus 1885, 93)

fourth Bishop of Antioch, Ignatius, in 107. Theophilus became the sixth bishop of Antioch.

Historical Setting

During the time Theophilus of Antioch was bishop, Marcus Aurelius (121-180) was the sixteenth Emperor of the Roman Empire. This emperor reigned between 161-180. During his reign many Christians were martyred, notably Justin and Polycarp. Theophilus became the sixth bishop of Antioch, succeeding Eros in 168. There is some controversy over the date of Theophilus' death, however, with some reports showing it as late as 188, with others a few years earlier. Theophilus wrote about the death of Marcus Aurelius, so it can be inferred to have occurred sometime after the death of that Roman Emperor in 180. The next recorded Bishop of Antioch was appointed in 188.

Marcion (of Sinope)

Theophilus was among other great Apostolic Fathers and apologists of the second century, though his reputation is not as distinguished as some of his contemporaries. Justin Martyr (b. 100) preceded Theophilus, dying in 165, and one of Justin's famous disciples, Tatian (b. 110, died ca. 172) is famous for writing the *Diatessaron*, which was one of the first attempts to harmonize the four Gospels into one work.

Theophilus came into his bishopric soon after Marcion of Sinope's death in 160. Marcion (b. 85) followed in the footsteps of his own father in becoming a bishop of Sinope; however, Marcion would be remembered for a more sinister belief system. Being unable to reconcile the God of love in the New Testament with the God of wrath in the Old Testament, Marcion espoused the belief that they were not the same God. Further, Marcion believed, because of the teachings and evidence of the life of Jesus, Jesus was truly the savior and represented the New Testament God as being the true God. Consequently, Marcion discounted most, if not all, of the Old Testament, and denied the authority of much of the New Testament as well. Only the Gospel of Luke was considered accurate (though absent any Old Testament references to Jesus), and ten epistles from the Apostle Paul were to be considered trustworthy.

Marcion's teachings were a source of grave concern among the Christian church both prior to and during Theophilus' time. Marcion gathered a large number of followers to his beliefs, and he had been excommunicated by Rome in 144. Other apologists of the second century, like Theophilus, would attack and condemn Marcion's teachings, which outlived their teacher.

Another heretic of the second century of which Theophilus would be forced to engage was Hermogenes who lived in the area of Carthage near the end of the second century into the first part of the third. Hermogenes believed and taught that the world was created from pre-existent matter. Specifically, his

154

argument consisted of three possible mechanisms for creation. Hermogenes reasoned that either 1) God made creation by dividing His substance, 2) God made creation out of nothing, or 3) God created from pre-existent matter. Hermogenes argued that God was immutable (unchangeable) and indivisible and therefore rejected the first possibility. He also argued that the presence of evil was evidence to reject the second possibility, that God made creation out of nothing. If God is good, and made everything perfectly, then evil would not exist, as it would imply a defect on God's creative ability. With the rejection of these two possibilities, Hermogenes thereby embraced the remaining option of God creating, like an architect or builder, from preexistent materials. The evil, or any imperfections, would therefore not be attributable to God, but be a result of the imperfections already present within the pre-existing matter.[188]

Writings

Theophilus is credited with writing numerous books, though only three have survived. The missing books are mentioned by Jerome and Eusebius. Jerome credits Theophilus with writing the apology *Against Marcion*, as well as commentaries on the Book of Proverbs and a harmony of the Gospels. Another book defending Christianity Theophilus was credited with authoring was *Against the Heresy of Hermogenes*, a book referred to by both Eusebius and Jerome. Theophilus refuted Hermogenes and contended for the position that God created out of nothing (referred to in theological terms as creation *ex nihilo*). Tertullian later joined Theophilus in rebutting Hermogenes, and there are accounts that

---

[188] (Wace 1999, 980)

Origen joined them within the first half of the third century.

The surviving books of Theophilus are part of the set *To Autolycus*. This three-volume work was a written, persuasive work apparently directed toward the salvation of Autolycus. Theophilus confessed in the beginning of his second book he was not gifted as a great orator: "...I am desirous, though not educated to the art of speaking, of more accurately demonstrating, by means of this tractate, the vain labour and empty worship in which you are held..."[189] This writing style may also be categorized as *protreptic* literature. *Protrepsis*, according to Rick Rogers, "was practiced by orators in the political arena and used by Aristotle and the Sophists, [and] was designed to recruit students to join a school or to accept a set of teachings as normative for their lives."[190] The three volumes were amidst gaps in time, and depicted a growing relationship between Theophilus and Autolycus in the series.

In the first book, Theophilus and Autolycus appeared to be more adversarial. Autolycus had apparently referred to Theophilus derogatively as a "Christian," a title that Theophilus happily accepted and provided reasons why he considered it a symbol of pride. Theophilus wrote, "...you call me a Christian, as if this were a damning name to bear..."[191] Theophilus, on the contrary, saw this title as a commissioning, because Christians were people anointed by the oil of God. Anointing was a common practice in this time.

---

[189] (Theophilus 1885, 94)

[190] (Rogers 2009, 218)

[191] (Theophilus 1885, 89)

Theophilus wrote, "...that which is anointed is sweet and serviceable, and far from contemptible."[192] For example, a house was anointed before it was made into a home. A ship was anointed prior to its first voyage. In like manner, a person becomes of service to God when he/she becomes anointed. A Christian, then, is one who has been anointed of the oil of God, and is therefore not contemptible, but rather is "sweet and serviceable." The role of a Christian was a noble calling, or as Paul referred to it in his second letter to the Corinthians, the anointed of God was that of an ambassador of Christ (2nd Corinthians 5:20).

In addition, the first book described the attributes and nature of God to Autolycus. Theophilus went further by illustrating the folly of idol worship, and the practice of worshipping the immoral gods that composed the Roman pantheon of gods. Theophilus was carefully laying out an argument why it was more reasonable to worship the un-created creator, rather than gods whittled out of a piece of wood, marble, or stone. Theophilus was not only providing positive reasons for his beliefs, but also denigrating the pagan beliefs simultaneously.

In his second work, Theophilus' writing took on a tone that was directed toward a more receptive reader. Theophilus referred to a former conversation with Autolycus concerning the latter's inquiries into Christianity, and, at the conclusion of that conversation the atmosphere was friendly. Theophilus wrote, "...having bid one another adieu, we went with much mutual friendliness each to his own house, although at first you had borne somewhat hard upon me."[193] This

---

[192] (Theophilus 1885, 92).

[193] (Theophilus 1885, 94)

second book then resumed from where the first ended, and Theophilus' goal was cited at the end of the first chapter: "I wish also, from a few of your own histories which you read, and perhaps do not yet quite understand, to make the truth plain to you."[194] This friendship would continue further into the third book described below.

The second book was focused toward one who was no longer hostile to the ideas of Christianity. It was written toward a person who was searching for the foundational issues of this belief system. Theophilus included in this book both a critique of the Grecian model for creation and provided a discourse from the first chapters of Genesis as a better, more reasonable explanation. Like in the first book, Theophilus was both demolishing the false ideologies and philosophies of the world, while at the same time providing a positive Biblical account as a more reasonable alternative. Of particular interest were the terms Theophilus used to describe the agents that created the world. He referred to God, His word (logos), and His wisdom (sophia). Theophilus never referred to the second person of the Trinity as Jesus, the "Son of God," or Christ. Despite this absence of a direct reference to Jesus, Theophilus does quote from the Gospel of John, who referred to Jesus in the opening verse as "The Word" (logos). In addition, since Jesus referred to the Father as "God," it is evident Theophilus was substituting logos for Jesus and sophia as the Holy Spirit.

In his third installment of this series written to Autolycus, Theophillus adopted a tone of a mentor tutoring a pupil. This book was a more intensive study

---

[194] (Theophilus 1885, 94)

into ethics and comparison with the pagan Greek/Roman morality. In this book Theophilus condemned the immorality of the Greek authors, but did so in a manner in which it was not directed specifically towards the reader (presumably Autolycus), but rather at the worldview in general. This further supports the idea that Autolycus was a person who was more prepared to learn the deeper concepts concerning Christianity, although at the time of the writing he remained unconverted.

Theophilus also addressed anti-Christian rumors that Autolycus apparently brought forth. By addressing these issues, Theophilus provided future readers a glimpse of the contemporary attitudes that non-believers held towards Christians. Rumors of the sharing of wives, incest (all Christians are "brothers and sisters in Christ"), and cannibalism ("unless you eat of the body of the Son of Man and drink his blood you will die in your sins") were addressed in this book. Theophilus even rebuked Autolycus for not being as skeptical of such slander as he was of the evidences Theophilus had brought forth concerning the truth of Christianity. Further, Theophilus provided numerous examples of these immoral accusations contained within the very worldview of Autolycus. He listed 1) Plato's ideal society in which all wives are common, 2) Epicurus' encouragement of incest with mothers and sisters, as well as 3) the precepts written by Zeno, Diogenes, and Cleanthes who commanded that fathers should be cooked and eaten by their own children. Theophilus denounced such practices and demonstrated, though the suggestion of these immoral acts were leveled at Christians, these accusations were actually the practice of the accuser's culture as depicted in the writings of the day.

This book focused upon the law of God as the rules that guide every person to salvation. Theophilus viewed the law as composed of four components, which were revealed through the Old Testament Prophets, Solomon's wisdom, the Gospels, and the letters of the Apostle Paul. The first component was repentance for transgressing the law given by God. Second was the need for righteousness, or justice in living. Jesus' golden rule provided in Matthew 7:12 epitomized this concept. The third component concerned chastity, including the topics of lust and divorce. And the fourth component, loving one's enemies, carried the second part a little farther. Again, Theophilus quoted from the Sermon on the Mount when he wrote "Love your enemies, and pray for them that despitefully use you. For if ye love them who love you, what reward have ye?"[195]

While Theophilus made no direct reference to Jesus, he did acknowledge the Gospel accounts when he wrote about Jesus' exposition of the law in the Sermon on the Mount. He wrote, "And the voice of the Gospel teaches still more urgently concerning chastity, saying: 'Whosoever looketh on a woman who is not his own wife, to lust after her, hath committed adultery with her already in his heart.'"[196]

Part of Theophilus' writing in *To Autolycus*, suggested a more legalistic approach to salvation. In his second book, Theophilus wrote,

> For as man, disobeying, drew death upon himself; so, obeying the will of God, he who desires is able to procure for himself life everlasting. For God has given us a law and holy commandments; and every one who

---

[195] (Theophilus 1885, 115)

[196] (Theophilus 1885, 115)

keeps these can be saved, and, obtaining the resurrection, can inherit incorruption.[197]

This approach suggested, given Theophilus' writing, that salvation was attainable through the keeping of the commandments. In the period directly following his work, both Jerome and Eusebius applauded this writing. Jerome (347-420) commended Theophilus' writings as "...well fitted for the edification of the church."[198] Apparently, this later church father did not think Theophilus' books were heretical or too legalistic. Eusebius (ca. 260 - 340), likewise did not condemn Theophilus' writings, though he critiqued them as "elementary treatises" in his *Ecclesiastical History*, suggesting the work was accurate, yet more appropriate for a beginning Christian. Given the apparent purpose behind the writing of these books, a basic approach to the tenets of Christianity was appropriate for Autolycus to gain an understanding. The books appear to have served this purpose.

Teachings

Theophilus' teachings are not well-known, save through his writings. It is reasonable, however, to believe he taught his congregation these same concepts in his role of Bishop of Antioch. Some scholars have accused Theophilus of being a "Jewish-Christian" because of the stress he appeared to have placed upon obedience to the law as a means of salvation. Evidence of such a position is contained within *To Autolycus* as described above.

However, with the admiration of Jerome and the affirmation of Eusebius, there are good reasons for not

---

[197] (Theophilus 1885, 105)

[198] (Jerome 1892, 369)

categorizing Theophilus as *nomistic*, a "works-based" theology from the Greek word *nomos* (law). Critics point to the absence of both the passion of Jesus and the concept of the substitutionary atonement within Theophilus' surviving books. Perhaps contained within his missing works were these foundational tenets of Christianity that were the cornerstone of the first century apostles. Perhaps Eusebius and Jerome, who were privy to Theophilus' lost writings, had evidence unavailable to today's scholars.

While Hermogenes was teaching God created from pre-existing matter, we see from Theophilus' writings that he taught a contrary view. In his first book, Theophilus wrote, "...all things God has made out of things that were not into things that are, in order that through His works His greatness may be known and understood."[199] This teaching was consistent with the other noteworthy theologians who regarded all of creation to have been created out of nothing.

Notably, Theophilus was credited with being the first to refer to the Godhead as the *trias* (triad or threesome), and he referred to the three persons as "God and his logos and his sophia." This concept was later developed and put forth as the Trinity by Tertullian, who articulated them as Father, Son, and Holy Spirit.

Conclusion

Theophilus provides us a glimpse into the rumors and allegations against Christianity in the early days of the church. While claiming to not be well trained as an orator in a culture that favored such skill, Theophilus provides us with valuable testimony in his defense of the

---

[199] (Theophilus 1885, 90)

followers of Christ. He prided himself as a Christian, defining it as one who is "anointed by God." Only when a person or item is anointed is it fully commissioned to perform its duty. Being anointed as a Christian charged the believer with performing the duties assigned by God.

Much of Theophilus' surviving work, *To Autolycus*, appears to provide a recipe for salvation through the adherence of the fourfold law: repentance of crimes, righteous living, acting chastely, and loving one's enemies. This adherence might be more akin to the theology taught by James who believed a true Christian would manifest works as fruits of their salvation.

Theophilus also shed light on the cultural flaws of society and the Roman and Greek mythos. It was through this persuasive collection of writings to which Theophilus sought to persuade Autolycus to become a Christian. While Autolycus' conversion remains a mystery, we can see the evolution of the relationship between him and the writer through the series. In the first book, Autolycus was addressed as an antagonist. The second writing engaged him as a skeptic who was receptive to a hearing of the evidence. And the third treatise treated Autolycus as a seeker who was on the verge of becoming a Christian. Theophilus' works remain a valuable testimony as an example of the work of the early church fathers.

Bibliography

Jerome. "Lives of Illustrious Men." In *A Select Library of the Nicene and Post-Nicene Fathers of the Christian Church, Second Series Volume III*, by Philip and Henry

Wace Schaff, 349-385. New York: Christian Literature Company, 1892.

Rogers, Rick. "Theophilus of Antioch." *Expository Times*, Feburary 2009: 214-224.

Theophilus, of Antioch. "Theophilus to Autolycus." In *The Ante-Nicene Fathers, Vol II: Hermas, Tatian, Athenagoras, Theophilus, and Clement of Alexandria*, by Marcus Dods, 85-122. Buffalo, NY: Christian Literature Company, 1885.

Wace, Henry. *A Dictionary of Christian Biography and Literature to the end of the sixth century.* Grand Rapids, MI: Christian Classics Ethereal Library, 1999.

CHAPTER 15 Irenaeus of Lyons - Against Heresies

Joel Furches

Early Life

Like most early Christian writers, information about Irenaeus's life is scarce and inexact. Most information about him either comes from what little can be gleaned from his writing, and from church tradition.

Irenaeus was born somewhere in the area of Smyrna. The exact date of his birth is a matter of conjecture. Some believe him to have been born between 115 and 125CE, while others will date his birth later, between 130 and 142CE. Irenaeus was apparently born into a Christian home and grew up in the church at Lyons where he was ordained a priest. During Irenaeus's childhood and young adulthood, he was privileged to hear the direct teachings of the elderly Polycarp, a former student of the Apostle John (both of whom are said to have lived into their 90's). The instructions of Polycarp apparently had a profound effect on Irenaeus, as he frequently cited these teachings in his writings.

While Irenaeus was serving as a priest, the church at Lyons encountered trouble with "Montanism," a heretical sect of self-proclaimed charismatic prophets. Irenaeus was dispatched to the church in Rome with a letter regarding Montanism, and with a glowing letter of introduction which labeled him, among other things, as "one zealous for the Testament of Christ." When Irenaeus returned from Rome, he discovered that his church had come under severe persecution, and that the bishop had been seized and killed. He found himself being elected the new bishop of Lyons.

While Irenaeus was bishop of Lyons, he labored diligently to evangelize the region. The largest obstacle to his efforts at evangelism was the rapid expansion of Gnosticism in Asia, and most of Irenaeus's diligence was poured into the effort to combat the corrupting effects of this heretical doctrine.

It was this project that prompted Irenaeus to author his *magnum opus* - a five-volume book entitled *Against Heresies*. This is widely considered to be the earliest known example of a systematic theology.

In the early 190's, Irenaeus was placed in the position of a peace-keeper when there was a difference of opinions between the church in Rome and the churches in Asia Minor concerning the observance of the Easter celebration. Irenaeus was successful at convincing the Roman church to lift the sentence of excommunication they had placed on the churches Irenaeus defended.

Irenaeus is believed to have died at the beginning of the third century. While tradition states that he was martyred, there is no concrete evidence for this.

Historical Setting

In the last half of the second century when Irenaeus lived, the Christian church was still rapidly expanding. With expansion came persecution, and martyrdom was still a very common way for Christians to meet their end.

Many Christian communities of the time viewed persecution and martyrdom to be a badge of honor as it showed their worthiness before the Lord. It was also widely considered to be a sign that Christ's return was almost upon them.

It is possibly this belief in the imminent return of Christ that had led to several difficulties: churches everywhere had not made any great efforts to gather and refine a definite cannon of scripture. The books of scripture were circulated throughout churches, but there was some disagreement on which books should be included, and most churches were not aware of all of the scriptural books in existence.

There was also at this time a high regard for the oral traditions passed down from the teachings of the apostles. As often as not it was these teachings that ministers cited in their preaching of the Gospel.

Finally, there had not been a great deal of effort put into nailing down systematic theologies to which everyone could refer, and most of the doctrines of the church were still being hashed out among the contemporary thinkers.

It was in this milieu that the heresy of Gnosticism flourished. While there were a wide variety of Gnostic sects, most of them claimed to have secret knowledge passed down to them through the oral traditions of the Apostles. Several of them also had their own "gospels"; forgeries named after such biblical characters as Thomas, Judas, and Mary Magdalene.

Because the Gnostics claimed to have the same authoritative resources as the orthodox church, Christian leaders such as Irenaeus were forced to trace the chain of custody of apostolic truths, and to define which scriptures were canonical and which were forgeries.

It was during this time period that great Christian writers and thinkers began to seriously devote themselves to the task of identifying false teaching as distinct from scriptural teachings.

Writings

It is uncertain how many works Irenaeus authored. Eusebius refers to four of his works that are now lost: *On the Ogdoad*, an untitled letter to Blastus regarding schism, *On the Subject of Knowledge* (also titled *On Science*), *On the Monarchy* (also titled *How God is not the Cause of Evil*). Only two of his books survive to this day: *The Demonstration of the Apostolic Preaching* (also known as *Proof of the Apostolic Preaching*), and *Against Heresies*.

Against Heresies (also titled *On the Detection and Overthrow of the So-Called Gnosis*) is by far his most influential work, as it brilliantly details the Gnostic teaching of the time, gives an excellent defense of the legitimacy of the four canonical gospels as well as many of the epistles, lays down a definite chain of custody for the apostolic teachings, and provides the first known (and very thorough) systematic theology.

Against Heresies has had a permanent effect on church doctrine ever since, and is a vital tool to modern apologists, as it is proof positive of the early dating of the gospels - especially the most criticized gospel, *John* - and of the chain of custody from the eyewitnesses of Jesus to the early church fathers.

Iranaeus wrote in a time before there was a universally recognized cannon of scripture. In *Against Heresies*, typically dated around 180CE, Iranaeus references the four recognized gospels, and all of the apostolic writings except *Philemon*, *James*, *2 Peter*, *2* and *3 John*, and *Revelation*. In so doing, he provides valuable evidence of the early adoption of these works as authoritative.

Against Heresies is a five volume work. In the first volume, Irenaeus gives a very thorough outline of the teachings of Gnosticism. In his 2009 lecture on Irenaeus, Professor Lawrence Feingold makes the point that to define Gnosticism was to refute it, since a bird's eye view of this "mystery cult" makes it obvious just how ridiculous their doctrine was.

Indeed, Irenaeus defines the Gnostic teachings with whit and sarcasm. For example, when explaining how the Gnostics taught that the waters of the earth came from the tears of the demigod Sophia, he adds that the Gnostics haven't taken into account the difference between the types of water in the earth. He suggests that they refine their teachings such that the *salt water* comes from her tears, and the *fresh water* from her sweat. He then winkingly suggests that his readers may imagine for themselves from whence the hot and acrid waters of the earth might spring.

Some scholars contend that Irenaeus's characterization of Gnosticism was occasionally exaggerated and that some of his sources were out of date. That said, he still appears to be masterfully well-informed on the subject he is addressing, and his work is still the best record that remains of these teachings.

The second book in *On Heresies* attempts to use pure reason to deconstruct the Gnostic doctrines, showing how they self-destruct under scrutiny. This is a useful book because in some senses it is a Presuppositional apologetic, inferring that reason and truth are grounded in God's nature and that, properly utilized, they will always ultimately prove God.

In book three, Irenaeus compares Gnostic teachings - which claim to be the true Christian doctrine - against scripture to show how scripture contradicts Gnostic claims. This comparison is so thorough and well-written, it could be argued that Irenaeus here provides the grounds for the rejection of all future heresies.

Book four focuses specifically on the teachings of Jesus, comparing them with the doctrine of the Old Testament to show that they are consistent with one another. Once again, Irenaeus provides an essential tool for future apologists, as the claim that the Old Testament is incompatible with the New Testament is a persistent one up to the current day.

Finally, book five compares Christ's teaching with the writings of the Apostle Paul to show that the two are in harmony. Throughout the history of the church, there have always been those who claim that Paul's doctrine and Christ's were different. By presenting this argument, Iranaeus has left a legacy that modern-day theologians would do well to adopt.

Against Heresies goes above and beyond its intended goal of refuting Gnosticism, and provides Christians everywhere with a systematic theology and a comprehensive foundation to errant claims of every type.

Teachings

Doctrine of Scriptural Authority

Irenaeus was a student of Polycarp who in turn was a student of the Apostle John who was a direct eyewitness of Jesus, his deeds and teachings. As such, Irenaeus was a third-hand hearer of the teachings of Jesus. In addressing the Gnostic's claim that they had a secret oral tradition passed down from the Apostles, Irenaeus challenged them to produce a chain of custody to the Apostles, and then proceeded to do just that for the church at Rome, listing the twelve bishops who had led the Roman church, beginning from the time that Peter and Paul taught together in Rome, up to his present day.

In his book *Our Legacy*, Dr. John Hannah defines Irenaeus's argument thusly:

> In the emergence of the bishop's office, Irenaeus was important because he appears to have been the first to attribute to church leaders a special custodial relationship to the truth – a notion unknown to Ignatius, Tertullian, or Origen. A line in Irenaeus's writings, referring to the bishops, states "Those who together with the succession of the episcopate, have received the certain gift of truth..." (*Against Heresy* 4:26). By this time, the bishop was viewed not merely as the head of a local church but also as an incorruptible guardian of the truth, because he was a part of the single episcopate emanating from the apostles. It was neither the office of the bishop nor his historical lineage that conferred authority on the leadership in the churches at this time; rather, it was the message and its conformity to the teachings of the apostles. Irenaeus wrote, 'True knowledge is [that which consists in] the doctrine of the apostles... according to the succession of the bishops... without any forging of Scriptures... a lawful and diligent exposition in harmony with the Scriptures' (*Against Heresy* 4:33).

-*Our Legacy*, Dr. John Hannah, p.44

This teaching becomes a double-edged sword. On the one hand, it provides valuable evidence against the claim of modern liberal scholars that the books of the New Testament are a series of haphazardly selected mythologies and forgeries thrown together by Constantine in the fourth century in order to control the gullible masses.

On the other hand, it has evolved into the foundation of the Catholic doctrine of the papacy and its claim to have Apostolic authority equal to that of scripture:

> For with [the Church in Rome], because of its superior origin, all churches must agree, that is, all the faithful in the whole world, and it is in her that the faithful everywhere have maintained the Apostolic Tradition

-Against Heresies 3.3.2

Doctrine of God

The Gnostic teachings on God were convoluted to say the least. With a complex series of "eons" (demigods) with interweaving origins and relationships one to another, Irenaeus was forced to outline the character of God, and his relationship to Christ Jesus, in no uncertain terms.

In the fourth book of *Against Heresies*, Irenaeus responded to the arguments of Marcion that the God of the Old Testament was a hateful and wrathful character that should be rejected in preference to the God of the New Testament. Irenaeus stresses that the God of the Old and New Testaments were the same, and that the concepts of justice and redemption are clearly shown throughout both Testaments.

In so-doing, Irenaeus took up the thread of John's Gospel, affirming the deity and humanity of Jesus and showing that Christ was of the same substance and the manifestation of God in flesh:

> There is therefore... one God the Father, and one Christ Jesus our Lord... in every respect, too, he is man, the formation of God: and thus he took up man into himself, the invisible becoming visible, the impassible becoming capable of suffering, and the Word being made man, thus summing up all things in himself

-Against Heresies III.16

The Doctrines of Sin and Redemption

Irenaeus said that Adam was created in the image of God with rational thought and free will:

> In man as well as in angels, he has placed the power of choice... so much so that those who had yielded obedience might justly possess what is good, given indeed by God, but preserved by themselves. On the other hand, they who have not obeyed... judgment: for God did kindly bestow on them what was good; but they themselves did not diligently keep it... Rejecting therefore the good... they shall all incur the just judgment of God.

- Against Heresies 4.37.1

Adam voluntarily disobeyed, corrupting the human race:

Through the disobedience of that one man... the many were made sinners and lost life

-Against Heresies 3.18.7

Christ restored to humanity what was lost through Adam (a restitutional view):

He summed up in Himself the long roll of the human race, bringing to us a compendious salvation, that what we lost in Adam, being in the image and likeness of God, we regained in Christ Jesus

- Against Heresies 3.18.1

...and the essence of Christ's work was substitutionary:

Redeeming us by His own blood in a manner consonant to reason, [He] gave Himself as a redemption for those who have been led into captivity... The Word of God, powerful in all things, and not defective with regard to His own justice, did righteously turn against that apostasy, and redeem from it His own property... Since the Lord thus has redeemed us through His own blood, giving His soul for our souls, and His flesh for our flesh... all the doctrines of the heretics fall to ruin.

-Against Heresies 5.1.1

Quite apparently, Irenaeus lays out a well-argued and circumspect doctrine of original sin, free will, and salvation:

Indeed, through the first Adam, we offended God by not observing His command. Through the second Adam, however, we are reconciled, and are made obedient even unto death. For we were debtors to none other except to Him, whose commandment we transgressed at the beginning

-Against Heresies 5.16.3

Doctrine of the Church

Irenaeus saw the church as the "Children of Abraham." Since Israel had never fully received the promise of a land; that promise had passed to Abraham's spiritual children - the church - in the future return of Christ.

As discussed above, Irenaeus was arguing against those who claimed to hold a secret knowledge outside what the orthodox church believed. Irenaeus responded with an argument that held that the orthodox church was a receptacle of the sacred truth passed down from the Apostles, and that the church in Rome was superior because it had been founded by Peter and Paul, consequently all other Christian churches must calibrate their teachings to that of Rome.

Doctrine of Eschatology

Irenaeus divided history up into seven different thousand-year epics (representing the seven days of the creation week). He believed himself to be living in the sixth epic, a time of trial and persecution leading to the revelation of the anti-Christ. The subsequent defeat of the anti-Christ, and the thousand-year-reign of Jesus that follows, he believed to be the final epic, symbolizing

God's Sabbath at the end of creation. After the millennial reign of Christ, the earth would be destroyed, the final resurrection of the dead would occur, and the creation of the new heaven and the new earth would usher in the eternal state.

Conclusion

The arguments for the truth of scripture and the revelations contained therein have not greatly changed over the centuries, and this is a good thing. If Christianity is the revelation of God and the only true worldview, then it does not require new proofs or arguments. In fact, if the arguments for the truth of Christianity had radically changed over the years, this would point to a system of belief that was untrue as it constantly had to adjust and evolve.

This being the case, it is worth the while of modern Christians to acquaint themselves with the classic arguments and proofs provided by the church fathers, and one could do little better than to read Irenaeus. Not only is his reasoning sound and scripturally grounded, but he is surprisingly readable for a man who wrote eighteen-hundred years ago.

CHAPTER 16 Origen—Zealous for the Church

Kyle J. Clark

"There is no man to whom the Church of Christ owes a more awful debt of reparation than to this incomparable saint, who [...] rendered to her greater services than all her other teachers—from whom in fact those teachers for many centuries derived an immense part of their knowledge and their thoughts..."[200]

Bishop Lightfoot (1828-1889), Bishop of Durham, echoes these comments about Origen of Alexandria when he said, "A deep thinker, an accurate grammarian, a most laborious worker, and a most earnest Christian, he not only laid the foundation, but, to a very great extent, built up the fabric of Biblical interpretation."[201] Origen was an early church father who published the first work on systematic theology and was the first to practice the art of textual criticism. Origen was an earnest learner of Christianity, and was one of the finest defenders of the faith. Origen was, at an early age, zealous for the Church.

Early Life and Ministry

Origen was born in Alexandria in approximately 185. He was the oldest of seven children and, while young, developed an early interest in Christianity through the teaching of his father Leonides. Origen proved to be an eager pupil of the Scriptures, and his

---

[200] (Farrar 1886, 187-88).

[201] (Farrar 1886, 188).

father was very proud of his learning. According to Eusebius, Origen was trained extensively on grammar, mathematics, philosophy, and Christianity and his father particularly drilled him to learn and recite his sacred studies on a daily basis. When he was seventeen, Origen's father was martyred in around 202. As would be expected, this event afflicted Origen and motivated him boldly to contend against his father's opponents regarding Christianity. He hoped to be found worthy of emulating his father in death as well as in life, and it was only through his mother's intervention that kept Origen from also finding martyrdom at a young age. Some accounts reflect that his mother hid Origen's clothing to thwart his intention to follow in the footsteps of his father, actively pursuing his own death at the hands of his father's persecutors. Whatever her method, his mother's attempt to keep Origen home were successful and led him to intensely study literature and *philology*, or the study of languages.

With the absence of his father, Origen assumed responsibility to help his family to survive. Alexandria was well known throughout the world as a literary arts center, and Origen utilized his writing skills to provide for his family. At the age of eighteen, Origen taught grammar initially, but, later, in response to questions from non-believers interested in Christianity and with the permission of the Bishop of Alexandria, he began teaching about Christianity as well. This passion for teaching about Christianity led to even more formal instruction in this area. The popularity of his classes soon forced Origen to divide his pupils, allowing the beginner students to be taught separately from the more mature Christians who received Origen's personal teaching in the more advanced topics.

Eusebius wrote that Origen came under the patronage of a wealthy woman in Alexandria, which may have also helped in the support of his family. Although her name remains unknown, Origen's willingness to stay with her suggests she was a Christian. Her other protégé, however, was notably not a follower of Jesus and this is evident in the report Eusebius provided. Origen's counterpart, Paul, a heretic, was well-skilled in arguments, and presented a significant challenge to Origen's views and followers. Eusebius related that the heretical Paul not only dissuaded some true Christians away from the Christian worldview, but also prevented many pagans from accepting the precepts of Christianity. Although young, Origen never wavered in his beliefs or his defense of the church. Eusebius wrote that Origen would not pray with Paul as this act would have compromised the believer's premise from the Apostolic Constitutions (VIII.34): "let not the godly pray with an heretic." Moreover, Origen zealously contended for the precepts and truths of Christianity, winning to him admiration and philosophical respect from around the region.

Origen studied philosophy under Ammonius Sacca (175? – ca. 242) for eleven years, and studied theology under Clement of Alexandria (150-215), ultimately succeeding Clement as a teacher upon Clement's retirement in 203. Both of these topics proved useful to Origen in his teachings as well as in his skills in the defense of the Christian worldview. In addition, to better understand the Old Testament, Origen learned the language of Hebrew. This enhanced his skills in the exegesis, or interpretation, of the Old Testament, and it also better enabled him to present his teachings on Jesus in light of the Scriptures. These skills became all the more evident in his adult life in his writings concerning the Old

Testament and his response to contemporary heretics. Origen would eventually write numerous commentaries, or explanations, of numerous Old Testament writings.

Eusebius reported that Origen voluntarily castrated himself to become a eunuch to teach better fellow Christians. Origen's motivation was from Matthew 19:12: "For there are eunuchs, who have been so from birth, and there are eunuchs who have been made eunuchs by men, and *there are eunuchs who have made themselves eunuchs for the sake of the kingdom of heaven*. Let the one who is able to receive this receive it" (ESV *emphasis added*). As Origen was teaching both men and women, he may have become a eunuch for the sake of proclaiming the Gospel of Christ. Regardless of the veracity of this claim, the contemporaries of Origen certainly felt this act was consistent with the zeal he had for the church.

In the first 250 years of Christianity, persecution of Christians was intermittently practiced within the Roman Empire. Like the waves of the ocean that ebb and flow, so did the attacks against Christians likewise occur in the first three centuries. When a wave of persecution was occurring, like during most of the life of Origen, few people dared teach about the Christian worldview. Origen, however, rose to the challenge and taught many, including Plutarch and his brother, Heracles (Heraclides). Plutarch, a name shared with a Roman historian of the first century, was martyred in approximately 202, while his brother, Heracles, later became the bishop of Alexandria. Thus heathens, who desired to learn more about Christianity, were drawn to Origen as he boldly proclaimed the teachings of Jesus despite the opposition of the secular authorities. The respect for Origen among Christian heretics and pagans may have been instrumental of his toleration by Roman officials despite his beliefs and teachings. It is believed Porphyry (c. 234-305), a Neo-Platonist who spoke out against Christians, may have been an acquaintance of Origen. Such was the respect of this early third century theologian.

Historical Setting

Origen's life coincided with some of the earlier persecutions faced by the church. Emperor Septimus Severus became emperor in 193, and he was an emperor who prohibited conversions to Christianity. While Severus' predecessors had not been as strict in the enforcement of the mandatory Roman worship practices, Christians had merely been provided a temporary reprieve. Severus took a more legalistic stance and authorized aggressive enforcement of Roman religious requirements throughout his reign. This wave of persecution, which took the life of Origen's father, lasted up until the end of Severus' reign, which ended in 211.

In conjunction with the persecutions permitted under Severus, Alexandria also had an ardent official who happily persecuted Christians. Aquila, the governor of Alexandria, was responsible for the arrest and martyrdom of many of Origen's pupils, including Plutarch, named above. Origen, however, was not intimidated by these acts and boldly encouraged the martyrs as they faced their deaths. He is reported to have walked among them and kissed them in tribute for their bravery, often inviting the anger of governing officials.

With the persecutions taking place among professing Christians, teachers such as Origen were rare. In fact, Origen may have been the only one brave enough to teach boldly about Christ in an area where Christian persecution was rampant. A brother of Plutach, Heracles, rose from being one of Origen's students to becoming a teacher under Origen. When his students became numerous, Origen tasked Heracles with teaching the more elementary topics to new believers, to allow Origen to teach the more advanced subjects.

In this period, Gnosticism continued to challenge the precepts of Christianity. Origen was an ardent defender against Gnosticism, and readily employed his philosophical training to refute the heretical claims of Gnostics in his day. Celsus was one such heretic whom Origen spoke against publicly, and Origen's defense of Christianity is remembered through one of Origen's published works titled *Contra Celsum*, or *Against Celsus*.

Writings

Origen has been referred to as the first New Testament textual critic, and was certainly one of the first biblical scholars. Jerome credited Origen with approximately eight hundred writings, though it may be much higher as Eusebius credits two thousand writings to Origen's credit, and Epiphanius credits up to eight thousand. Not many of these writings remain in existence today; partly this is the result of a sixth century condemnation of some of Origen's views, but mostly it is a result of the age of the writings.

One of his greatest works was the *Hexapla*, a publication consisting of six columns of the Old Testament that took Origen twenty years to compile. The six columns designated the format of the book. The first column was in Hebrew, a second column was the Greek transliteration of the Hebrew where Origen phonetically spelled the sounds of the Hebrew words into Greek, and a third column was the Septuagint, the most widely accepted Greek version of the Old Testament. The remaining three columns were Greek versions of the Old Testament written by second century translators Symmachus, Aquila of Sinope, and Theodotion. This arrangement provided an early version of textual criticism and allowed readers to compare the differing versions of the text. The Septuagint portion sometimes omitted portions contained within the Hebrew version, and yet sometimes added material that was not contained within it as well. With his knowledge of Hebrew, Origen was able to identify the extra passages with an obelus (÷), and the omitted passages which he re-inserted were identified with an asterick (*). Similar practices on identifying spurious passages are still in practice among textual critics today. Unfortunately, Origen's Hexapla was not copied sufficiently and fell out of existence, though many of the versions of the Greek Old Testament did survive. To complicate the issue, the identifying marks inserted by Origen to identify the variations between texts were omitted from later copies. As a result, copies of the Septuagint derived from Origen's Hexapla inadvertently became contaminated because the insertions were not identified in later manuscripts, and these were passed down in the church mistakenly as the original Septuagint writings.

Another of Origen's writings of renown was *De Principiis*, or "On First Principles." This book was the first book comprising a systematic theology in the Christian church. It blended Origen's knowledge of Greek philosophy with his knowledge of Christianity. It was through this book that much of Origen's teachings were recorded and his belief system was articulated for others to read and gain a better understanding of Christianity. Also entering into this book was Origen's lack of confidence in some Old Testament passages as being literally true, but these were reconciled through a strong belief in allegory to hold to the principal of inerrancy of Scripture. To Origen, certain parts of the Old Testament might not be physically and historically accurate, yet when accepted as an allegory, the passages could remain truthful. Origen believed that the Bible was divinely inspired, yet it was not always to be interpreted literally. Origen believed that, just as man is body, soul, and spirit, so also the Bible is literal, moral, and allegory. In this light, for example, Origen accepted the days of creation as allegory, as the idea that the first three days would have been without sun, moon, and stars seemed ludicrous to him and therefore the creation account must also be considered in an allegorical sense.

One of the greatest apologetic works produced by the early church was that in which Origen confronted the heretic Celsus. A Greek philosopher of the second century, Celsus wrote against Christianity in *The True Word* around the year 178. Celsus believed 1) the Old Testament did not truly reflect predictions of events of the coming Christ, though this objection was ultimately a tacit admission that the events these prophecies predicted had indeed been fulfilled. Celsus also alleged 2) the fulfillments of prophecy concerning the Messiah were nothing short of falsehoods created to encourage people to believe in Jesus. Further, 3) any miracles attributed to Jesus were, according to Celsus, nothing short of legends of his greatness or of his skill as a sorcerer. Further. Celsus asserted 4) the resurrection was merely a borrowing of pagan mythology. And finally, Celsus claimed 5) any truths contained within the Bible, or points of wisdom, were actually ideas smuggled in from Greek philosophy. *The True Word* was an early and significant philosophical challenge to the precepts of the Christian faith. No copies of this writing exist today, and it is only through Origen's writing that we know it even existed.

Origen, publicly and literally, refuted Celsus point by point. The writing that came from this defense of Christian doctrine was *Against Celsus*, and was published around 248. Origen demonstrated proof of how the Old Testament could not have been manufactured at a later date, and Origen was one of the first to utilize the conversions of Paul, along with the satisfaction of Thomas' doubts, as proof of the bodily resurrection of Christ. Origen utilized his skills in philosophy to persuade his listeners and readers of the truth of the Christian worldview. One additional charge he refuted in this work was the accusation that Christians were not true citizens because they refused military service. Origen disagreed. He famously quoted "We who by our prayers destroy all demons which stir up wars, violate oaths, and disturb the peace are of more help to the emperors than those who seem to be doing the fighting."[202] Origen declared that Christians were actually the ones who were making the greatest victories on behalf of the Empire. Christians were eliminating the spiritual sources of conflicts.

Much of Origen's views concerning the Scriptures were captured in his numerous commentaries. From the Old Testament, Origen wrote commentaries on Genesis, Psalms, the Song of Songs, the book of Lamentations, and

---

[202] (Galli 2000, 334).

the prophets. From the New Testament writings, Origen wrote commentaries on Matthew, John, and the many writings from the Apostle Paul. Origen also wrote homilies, or sermon-like discourses, on sections of Scriptures as well. These discourses were written primarily on the Old Testament from portions of Genesis, Exodus, Leviticus, Numbers, Joshua, Judges, Ruth, 1 Samuel, Song of Songs, Isaiah, Jeremiah, and Ezekiel. This was likely the result of his command of Hebrew and his knowledge of the Old Testament. Despite his commentaries on some of the books from the New Testament, the only homilies Origen is known to have written were from the Gospel of Luke.[203]

Some of Origen's writings also speak of the transformation process in which a believer progressed after conversion. This process, Origen wrote, began with the new believer in a relationship with the Father, which was based primarily upon fear. He likened this with the slave, or servant, relationship with a master. Over time, as the believer comes to know the Father, this relationship progresses into one that is more like a son to a father; a relationship based upon love rather than upon fear. Reinhartz sums up Origen's idea: "…as the believer comes to know God as Father, the believer advances from the status of servant to that of disciple, from disciple to infant, from infant to brother of the Son, and so becomes a son of God."[204] This progression was made manifest through the moral behavior of the believer. To support his view, Origen called upon the Apostle John and his first epistle "No one born of God makes a practice of sinning, for God's seed abides in him, and he

---

[203] (Cabaniss 1992).

[204] (Reinhartz 2001, 113).

cannot keep on sinning because he has been born of God" (1 John 3:9 ESV). Therefore, for a person to progress from servant to son it must be in accordance with obedience to the Word of God.

Many of Origen's writings also reflected his views concerning the allegory, or "Spiritual interpretation" of Scriptures. As man was three parts – body, soul and spirit, and God was three parts – Father, Son, and Holy Spirit, then the Scriptures must also be viewed in like manner. As mentioned above, there were many accounts within these writings Origen had difficulty coming to terms with, and the use of allegory was a method that allowed him to maintain his view of the inerrancy of Scripture. Examples of his understanding, he believed, could be found in the Gospel accounts. For example, the Gospels of Matthew and Luke could be viewed as comparable to the bodily form of Christ. The Gospel of Mark, on the other hand, would be more akin to the Jesus of prophecy, or the soul of Christ. Finally, the Gospel of John was the spirit of Jesus.

It was Origen's writings on the allegorical interpretation of Scripture that later caused the church to reject Origen's ideas and writings. Centuries later, the Emperor Justinian would declare anathema many of the teachings of Origen, which only survived at this point in writing. In the fifth ecumenical council, which convened in 553, many of Origen's non-Scripturally based teachings were declared heretical. Specifically, in the writings that survived, the notions that there was a preexistence of the soul, in which Origen believed souls existed prior to earthly life, and the idea of universalism, that everyone will ultimately be saved, were found in his writings. Origen also wrote on the hierarchy of the Trinity, in which the three members of the Godhead were ranked in authority as Father, Son, and Holy Spirit, and, while affirming the resurrection of Jesus from the dead, Origen denied the permanent physical resurrection of Jesus. He wrote that Jesus' physical body was temporary for the appearances to the disciples and then it was later discarded and only the spirit of Jesus remains.

Defenders of Origen suggest the writings may have been corrupted between Origen's death and the mid-sixth century. Despite the original writing, those writings that survived attracted the attention of the fifth ecumenical council who declared, point by point, those teachings which were heretical. These declarations certainly marred the character of Origen, though much of his work was truly unparalleled for his time. His writings became the first systematic theology and the first apologetic defense for Christianity. Despite the controversy, some of his writings have survived.

Teachings

As described above, Origen began teaching grammar at an early age, and Christian theology soon after. He alone, or with perhaps few others, were bold enough to teach in defiance of Rome about Jesus Christ. Although not an ordained priest, Origen demonstrated a firm command of the tenets of Christianity, and the Bishop of Alexandria, Demetrius, appointed Origen to fill Clement of Alexandria's role as head of the catechetical school when Clement retired in 203. Origen was merely eighteen when he assumed this role.

Initially, Origen taught new converts the principles of catechism, which is the knowledge that prepared the prospective believers to be baptized into the faith. When the number of students began to grow, he designated one of his pupils to teach Christianity at the introductory level so that he could teach more advanced concepts and ideas to the mature Christians. Origen's fame began to spread outside of his home in Alexandria.

As his popularity grew among Alexandria, it appears jealousy may have arisen proportionately between Origen and Demetrius. Origen was often summoned to other areas to teach. When Origen's popularity spread to other parts of the Roman Empire, the jealousy became worse. During the reign of Alexander Severus, the Emperor's mother, Mamaea, summoned Origen to teach her about Christianity in Antioch. The prestige of educating the Emperor's mother regarding the precepts of Christianity encouraged Origen to go to her.

Origen's route to Antioch took him through Jerusalem and Caesarea where he was warmly welcomed and encouraged on his mission. His tension with his home bishop of Alexandria increased when the bishops of Jerusalem and Caesarea both allowed Origen to preach to the priests in their areas. Alexander, bishop of Jerusalem, and Theoctistus, bishop of Caesarea, were thrilled with Origen's mission to teach Mamaea. To further Origen's credibility, they ordained him into the priesthood. This act, done without consulting Origen's home bishop, infuriated Bishop Demetrius of Alexandria and he banished Origen from returning to Alexandria. Further, Demetrius sent out letters of condemnation to all of the churches concerning Origen in 232. While many churches upheld Origen's banishment, the churches in Palestine, Phoenicia, Arabia, and Achaea rejected this decree. Not to be deterred, Origen took up residence in Caesarea. It was there he continued his teaching and writing, under the patronage of Ambrose of Alexandria (d. 250) who was a former Marcionite and Gnostic who had become convinced by Origen's teachings regarding the truth of Christianity. Origen's internal persecution from Demetrius came to an end later the same year when Demetrius died in 232. Ironically, Eusebius reported that Bishop Demetrius was succeeded by one of Origen's star pupils, Heracles, upon Demetrius' death.

Conclusion

Origen was finally imprisoned during a new wave of persecution under the Emperor Decius around the year 251. Almost fifty years had transpired since the martyrdom of his father, and it appeared likely Origen was to experience the same fate. This delay of forty-eight years, however, brought about a greater good that Origen, as a seventeen year-old boy, could not have foreseen when he earnestly sought to by martyred with his father. His upbringing, coupled with his zeal for the church, brought forth the teachings and conversions of countless non-believers during periods of Roman persecution. Further, this nearly half-century provided him opportunity to author hundreds of writings that helped shape the Christian worldview into a systematic theology that provided consistency.

Origen was tortured while imprisoned. The Roman authorities under Emperor Decius hoped they could cause the 65 year-old Christian apologist to forsake his beliefs. Origen had waited his entire adult life for such an ordeal. When pressed to deny Christ, Origen refused. The Roman officials' hopes were dashed. Origen maintained his witness to Jesus, just like his father and his pupils had before him, and outlasted the Emperor. When Decius died in 252, Origen was set free. Despite his freedom, however, the physical ordeal he experienced during his imprisonment and torture greatly damaged his health. Slightly more than one year following his release, Origen died a follower of Jesus. Even unto death, Origen maintained his zeal for the church.

Bibliography

Cabal, Ted. "Notable Christian Apologist: Origen." In *The Apologetics Study Bibe: Real Questions, Straight Answers, Stronger Faith*, by Ted, Chad O. Brand, E. Ray Clendenen et. al Cabal, 1387. Nashville, TN: Holman Bible Publishers, 2007.

Cabaniss, A. "Origen (Origenes Adamantius)." In *Who's Who in Christian History*, by J.D., and Philip W. Comfort Douglas, 522. Wheaton, IL: Tyndale House, 1992.

Farrar, Frederic William. *History of Interpretation.* London: Macmillan and Co., 1886.

Galli, Mark and Ted Olsen. *131 Christians Everyone Should Know*. Nashville, TN: Christianity Today, Inc., 2000.

Gohl, Justin M. "Origen." In *The Lexham Bible Dictionary*, by ed. John D. Barry. Bellingham, WA: Logos Bible Software, 2012.

Reinhartz, Adele ed. *Semeia 85: Gof the Father in the Gospel of John*. Atlanta: Society of Biblical Literature, 2001.

CHAPTER 17 Constantine the Great - A Defender of Christianity?

Edward D. Andrews

Many Christian scholars have given Roman Emperor Constantine the expressions "saint," "thirteenth apostle," "holy equal of the apostles"; while others describe Constantine as "bloodstained, stigmatized by countless enormities and full of deceit, . . . a hideous tyrant, guilty of horrid crimes."

Numerous confessing Christians have long thought of Constantine the Great as the supreme advocate, who, in essence, was the savior of Christianity. It is to this man that most of today's Christian body attributes the delivery of Christianity from Roman persecution, releasing them from the bondage of being the outlaw religion, bringing them freedom from oppression.

Additionally, it is commonly thought that he was faithful and followed a life course as a follower of Jesus Christ with a resilient desire to spread the Christian cause. The Eastern Orthodox Church and the Coptic Church have avowed both Constantine and Helena, his mother, "saints."

Who was Constantine the Great? What role did he play in the growth of postapostolic Christianity? We will allow history and the historians to answer these questions.

In short, the reader will find that there is some truth and some untruth when it comes to Constantine the Great. It is true that he was a consummate benefactor of Christianity, but it is also untrue that he was a Christian. It is true that he was a zealous defender of Christianity, but it is also untrue that his life course was anything near reflective of being Christlike. We will allow the historical evidence and common sense to be the advocates of what is true, and what is untrue.

The Constantine of History

In Naissus, in Serbia about the year 275 C.E., there was a son born to Constantius Chlorus, whose name would be infamously known the world over as Constantine the Great. His father would become emperor of the western provinces of Rome in 293 C.E., at which time; Constantine was fighting on the Danube under the order of Emperor Galerius. In the year of 306 C.E., Constantine would have to return to his father's dying side in Britain, at which time the army raised him to the status of emperor.

At that point, there were five others laying hold of the title Agusti (Agustus singular). Between 306 and 324 C.E., subsequently Constantine became lone imperator, which was a time of incessant civil war. Constantine would have two substantial victories in two sets of campaigns, placing himself in world history, making him the sole emperor of the Roman Empire.

In 312 C.E., Constantine conquered his adversary Maxentius in the battle of the Milvian Bridge outside Rome. The Christian apologist assert that throughout that battle, there appeared under the sun a flaming cross carrying the Latin words In hoc signo vinces, meaning "In this sign conquer." Some also argue that in a dream, Constantine was commanded to paint the first two letters of Christ's name in Greek on the troop's shields. However, the story suffers from numerous chronological errors. The book A History of Christianity states: "There is a conflict of evidence about the exact time, place and details of this vision." (Johnson 1976, 167) Back in Rome, the pagan Senate, received Constantine openheartedly, who declared him, chief Augustus and Pontifex Maximus, that is, high priest of the pagan religion of the Roman Empire.

Constantine organized a relationship with Emperor Licinius, ruler of the eastern provinces, in 313 C.E. By way of the Edict of Milan, the two allowed all groups to worship freely, each having equal rights. However, numerous historians soften the meaning of this document, suggesting that it was no imperial document indicating a modification of procedure toward Christianity; rather, it was simply a routine official letter.

By 323 C.E., Constantine crushed his final lingering opponent, Licinius, and became the unquestionable ruler of the Roman world. Still unbaptized, in 325 C.E., he was the head of the first great ecumenical council of the "Christian" church, which judged Arianism as heresy and penned a statement of crucial beliefs called the Nicene Creed.

In the spring of 337 C.E., Constantine fell sick. It is at this point that he chose to be baptized, and then he died that 22nd of May. The senate placed him among the Roman gods after his death.

Constantine's Strategic use of Religion

There was a distinct attitude of the third and fourth century Roman Emperors. These ones may have not held the same position of the religion of the day, but they were politician enough to surrender to the mood of the times. Many times, they would bow to the religious movement ahead of their own agenda, giving the impression, regardless of how small, that they too were religious. Moreover, there is no doubt that Constantine was man of his day. At the start of making his mark, he needed some divine support, which would not come from the Roman gods, who were on their way out, as an influential agent.

The Roman Empire was on the brink of full deterioration. What it needed was a new breath of life, and what better than Christianity, which gave credence to his victory, but to a new empire that was just ahead. The Christian churches throughout the empire were now what held the empire together, looking to the bishops, requesting they keep the unity.

Constantine recognized Christianity for its worth, albeit divided amongst themselves, if he could effectively solve their differences, the empire could be revitalized and united into a new force, for his will and purposes. He decided to unite the people under one "catholic," or universal, religion. Pagan customs and festivals were given "Christian" names. In addition, "Christian" religious leaders were given position, salary, and dominant influence of pagan priests. (Durant 1980, 616)

Looking for religious accord for political motives, Constantine rapidly stamped out any nonconforming expressions, not based on Biblical truth, but based on majority agreement. The deep religious differences within the seriously divided Christian church afforded him the occasion to arbitrate as a God-sent negotiator.

By way of his relations with the Donatists in North Africa and the supporters of Arius in the eastern portion of the empire, he swiftly learned that persuading was not sufficient to establish a firm, unified reliance. The first ecumenical council in the history of the church came about by his attempt to resolve the Arian controversy.

Historian Paul Johnson has this to say concerning Constantine, "One of his main reasons for tolerating Christianity may have been that it gave himself and the State the opportunity to control the Church's policy on orthodoxy and the treatment of heterodoxy." (Johnson 1976, 87)

The Council of Nicaea and Constantine

The question is, what part did the unbaptized Constantine have at the Council of Nicaea? The Later Roman Empire states: "Constantine himself presided, actively guiding the discussions . . . Overawed by the emperor, the bishops, with two exceptions only, signed the creed, many of them much against their inclination." (Jones 1986, 87) For two months the religious debates went on, before this pagan emperor stepped in and determined that those who favored homoousion (of one substance). Why? "Constantine had basically no understanding whatsoever of the questions that were being asked in Greek theology," says A Short History of Christian Doctrine. (Lohse 1978, 51)

A Case for Hope states, "Constantine, who was not a member of the church, presided at the council and said in effect, 'I really don't care what you decide, but decide you will, and then I will make certain that the decision is enforced.'" (Kerby 2001, 73) Obviously, Constantine did understand that a religiously divided empire was a threat to the solidarity he was searching for, unity. "What religion he had, many argue, was at best a blend of paganism and Christianity for purely political purposes." (Galli and Olsen 2000, 306)

Constantine Became a Christian?

Johnson notes: "Constantine never abandoned sun-worship and kept the sun on his coins." (Johnson 1976, 87) Forgery in Christianity observes, "Constantine showed equal favour to both religions. As pontifex maximus he watched over the heathen worship and protected its rights." (Wheless 2007, 30) "First, Constantine never became a Christian himself until he was baptized on his death bed. Furthermore, his behavior as emperor was the antithesis of Christian principles." (Kerby 2001, 72) In fact, the day before his death, his being the Pontifex Maximus, Constantine made a sacrifice to Zeus. Therefore, it is only fair to ask concerning his baptism, 'was it preceded by sincere repentance and a turning around from his former way, as is required by Scripture. —Acts 2:38, 40, 41.

Family Murders

Under Constantine, Crispus and Fausta heading, Michael Grant describes what one could call repulsive domestic crimes committed by Constantine:

Eutropius declared that Constantine was responsible for many murders of his 'friends.' And this was unmistakably true. There was a long list of victims. . . . Constantine's behavior is inexcusable by any standards, and casts a blot on his reputation. Being an absolute autocrat, he believed that he could kill anyone. (Grant 2009, 109)

Not long after Constantine's dynasty was under way, he lost the ability at enjoying his accomplishments, as he was soon all too aware of the dangers that surrounded him. He was suspicious to start with, coupled further by those seeking to curry favor with him, nothing but disaster lay ahead. Suspicion came over his nephew Licinianus first. He had already executed Licinianus' father, who had been the co-Augustus. After Licinianus' murder, Constantine actually had his own firstborn son murdered, Crispus. It was Crispus' stepmother, who executed him, because he seemed to be in the way of her own offspring.

Fausta's plot was short lived, as this act sealed her own fate. Constantine's mother, Augusta Helena, murdered Fausta, or at least was involved in it. The irrational feelings that often exacted Constantine likewise contributed to the flood of executions of numerous friends and associates. The book An Introduction to Medieval Europe concludes: "The execution—not to say murder—of his own son and his wife indicates that he was untouched by any spiritual influence in Christianity." (Thompson and Johnson 1965, 32)

A "Saint"?

Philip Schaff states: "Constantine was entitled to be called Great in virtue rather of what he did than what he was. Tested by character, indeed, he stands among the lowest of all those to whom the epithet [Great] has in ancient or modern times been applied." (Schaff 1997, 18) And the book A History of Christianity informs us: "There were early reports of his violent temper and his cruelty in anger. . . . He had no respect for human life . . . . His private life became monstrous as he aged." (Johnson 1976, 47)

Obviously, Constantine had grave disposition problems. His unpredictable personality was frequently the cause for his committing crimes. Constantine certainly was not a Christian by nature. The evidences do not portray him as a real Christian who had put on "the new person" and who demonstrated that he had the fruitage of the Spirit—"love, joy, peace, patience, kindness,

goodness, faithfulness, gentleness, self-control."[205]—
Colossians 3:9, 10; Galatians 5:22, 23.

The Consequences of His Efforts

As Pontifex Maximus—and consequently the religious head of the Roman Empire—Constantine attempted to persuade the bishops of a church that had now fallen away. Christianity was now entering the realms of position, power and wealth for its leaders, by means of Constantine. While they were not the state religion at this point, it was certainly heading in that direction. Soon the church was ready to bestow titles on the man that had rained splendor down on them, angel of God, a sacred being, and looking to him as the Son of God, who would reign in heaven.

This Christianity was not the Christianity of the first and second century of our common era. It had chosen to become a part of the world, to such an extent, there was no difference. It had left the love it had at first, the teachings of Christ. (John 15:19; 17:14, 16; Revelation 17:1, 2) As a result, Christianity was fused with the world of government and paganism, as well as Neoplatonist.—Compare 2 Corinthians 6:14-18.

The church too would become authoritarian, by way of Constantine's early influence. The gospel was set aside for arrogant rites and ceremonies presented, with worldly honors and monetary payments for every priestly function. Moreover, the Kingdom of Christ was moved into becoming a kingdom of this world.

---

[205] W. Hall Harris, III, The Lexham English Bible (Logos Research Systems, Inc., 2010), Ga 5:21–23

CHAPTER 18 Jerome - The Forerunner in Bible Translation

Edward D. Andrews

The Catholic Church Sacred Tradition in support of the Vulgate's magisterial authority:

> Moreover, this sacred and holy Synod,— considering that no small utility may accrue to the Church of God, if it be made known which out of all the Latin editions, now in circulation, of the sacred books, is to be held as authentic,—ordains and declares, that the said old and vulgate edition, which, by the lengthened usage of so many years, has been approved of in the Church, be, in public lectures, disputations, sermons and expositions, held as authentic; and that no one is to dare, or presume to reject it under any pretext whatever.[206]

ON April 8, 1546, the Latin Vulgate was given an approved capacity by the Council of Trent (1545–1563) as the standard of the Biblical canon regarding which parts of books are canonical. The Vulgate had been completed for over a thousand years, yet Jerome and his translation had been the center of debate throughout. Who was Jerome? Why was his translation of the Hebrew and Greek Scriptures into Latin, as well as himself debated? What impact has this work had on the field of Bible translation?

---

[206] Canons and Decrees of the Council of Trent, The Fourth Session, 1546.

Jerome Becomes a Scholar

Jerome ([c. 346–420 C.E.] Latin: Eusebius Hieronymus) was a Roman Christian priest, confessor, theologian and historian, who became a Doctor of the Church. He was the son of Eusebius, of the city of Stridon, which was on the border of Dalmatia and Pannonia. His parents were reasonably well-off, and he felt the benefits of money at an early age, receiving an education in Rome under the well-known grammarian Donatus. Jerome demonstrated himself to be a exceptional student of grammar, rhetoric, and philosophy. Throughout this period he also began to study Greek. He is most famously known for his translation of the Bible from the original languages of Hebrew (OT) and Greek) (NT) into Latin (the Vulgate), and his list of writings is extensive.

Jerome was born at Stridon about 346 C.E. However, he was not baptized until sometime after close to 366 C.E, and shortly thereafter, he and his friend Bonosus headed for Rome. However, they became wanderers for a time, and then finally ended up in Aquileia, Italy, where Jerome was introduced to the idea of asceticism.[207] He became attracted to this extreme way of life, se he and a group of his friends spent a number of years cultivating an ascetic way of life.

In 373 C.E., some unnamed trouble contributed to the groups going their separate ways. Let down, Jerome traveled without a purpose and without a known destination eastward across Bithynia, Galatia, and Cilicia and eventually arrived in Antioch, Syria.

---

[207] self-denying way of life: austerity and self-denial, especially as a principled way of life

Even though he was only in his late 20's at this point, Jerome's health was damaged by a fever and he grew very ill during his journey. "Oh, if only the Lord Jesus Christ would suddenly transport me to you," he said, writing to a friend, Rufinus. "My poor body, weak even when well, has been shattered by frequent illnesses."[208]

Jerome had already coped with sickness, seclusion, and inner turmoil; he was now thrust into a spiritual crisis. In a dream, he was ...

Suddenly I was caught up in the spirit and dragged before the judgment seat of the Judge; and here the light was so bright, and those who stood around were so radiant, that I cast myself upon the ground and did not dare to look up. Asked who and what I was I replied 'I am a Christian.' But He who presided said: 'Thou liest; thou art a follower of Cicero and not of Christ. For where thy treasure is there will thy heart be also.' Instantly I became dumb, and amid the strokes of the lash—for He had ordered me to be scourged—I was tortured more severely still by the fire of conscience, considering with myself that verse 'In the grave, who shall give thee thanks?' Yet for all that I began to cry and to bewail myself saying: 'Have mercy upon me, O Lord; have mercy upon me.' Amid the sound of the scourges this cry still made itself heard. At last the bystanders, falling down before the knees of

---

[208] Jerome, "The Letters of St. Jerome", Volume VI: St. Jerome: Letters and Select Works, ed. Philip Schaff and Henry Wace (New York: Christian Literature Company, 1893), 4.

Him who presided, prayed that He would have pity on my youth, and that He would give me space to repent of my error. He might still, they urged, inflict torture upon me, should I ever again read the works of the Gentiles. Under the stress of that awful moment I should have been ready to make even still larger promises than these. Accordingly I made oath and called upon His name, saying 'Lord, if ever again I possess worldly books, or if ever again I read such, I have denied thee.' On taking this oath, I was dismissed, and returned to the upper world.[209]

Sometime later would sidestep his pledge that he had made in the dream, and said that he should not be held answerable for a solemn promise made in a dream.

---

[209] Rufinus of Aquileia, "The Apology of Rufinus", trans. William Henry Fremantle In , in A Select Library of the Nicene and Post-Nicene Fathers of the Christian Church, Second Series, Volume III: Theodoret, Jerome, Gennadius, Rufinus: Historial Writings, Etc., ed. Philip Schaff and Henry Wace (New York: Christian Literature Company, 1892), 462-63.

However, Jerome felt somewhat obligated to his vow, so he left Antioch and searched for solitude in Chalcis in the Syrian Desert. Living as a recluse, he submerged himself in a study of the Bible and theological literature. Jerome said, "I read the books of God with a zeal greater than I had previously given to the books of men."[210] He likewise learned the local Syriac tongue and started studying Hebrew with the help of a Jew who had become a Christian.

Jerome Receives an Assignment from the Pope

After about five years of living an ascetic life, Jerome returned to Antioch in 378 or 379 C.E. His return to civilization was met with disappointment, as the church was profoundly divided. While he had still been in the desert, Jerome had written to the Pope, saying "The church is rent into three factions, and each of these is eager to seize me for its own."[211]

Jerome eventually decided that he would take the side of Bishop Paulinus, one of three men that claimed that title of Antioch. Jerome unwilling accepted his being ordained, but demanded (1) that he not be held back from being able to continue his ascetic life, and (2) he would remain freed from any priestly duties to minister to a specific church.

---

[210] Jerome, "The Letters of St. Jerome", Volume VI: St. Jerome: Letters and Select Works, ed. Philip Schaff and Henry Wace (New York: Christian Literature Company, 1893), 36.

[211] Jerome, "The Letters of St. Jerome", Volume VI: St. Jerome: Letters and Select Works, ed. Philip Schaff and Henry Wace (New York: Christian Literature Company, 1893), 20.

Jerome went with Paulinus to the Council of Constantinople and afterward continued on with him to Rome in 381 C.E. Pope Damasus swiftly appreciated Jerome's learning and linguistic expertise. Inside of a year Jerome was raised to the important position of personal secretary to Damasus.

Once in the position of personal secretary, Jerome seemed to attract controversy at every turn. For example, even though he lived in a luxurious papal court, he continued in his ascetic lifestyle. This was not only frowned upon, but he even went a step further and spoke out against the excessive lifestyle of the worldly clergy, creating numerous enemies.

Regardless of those who despised him, Jerome had the complete backing of Pope Damasus. Of course, the pope had very good reasons for seeing that Jerome continued in his Bible research. The Latin Bible version, were really in numerous forms; as many of them had been carelessly translated, filled with errors. Another problem that Damasus faced was the division of his church, the East and the West. Few in the Eastern portion of the church knew Latin, and fewer still in the Western portion knew Greek.

Therefore, it was Pope Damasus' intention to have Jerome create a standard Latin text of the Gospels. Damasus desired a translation that would me a mirror image of the original language Greek texts, yet at the same time, be moving, stirring and powerful, as well as clear in the Latin. Jerome and only a handful of other scholar were up to such a task. He was fluent in Greek, Latin, and Syriac and possessed a fundamental knowledge of Hebrew, making him well suited for the job. Therefore, Jerome was commissioned into a project by

Damasus that would not be completed for the next 20 years of his life.

Greater Controversies Lie Ahead

Jerome was a translator with a mission, and it showed with the speed for which he was accomplishing his task. Jerome exhibited a clear, technique that would be used by translator and textual scholars over a millennium later. One of the leading textual scholars of the 20th century, the late Dr. Bruce M. Metzger had this to say about Jerome's method:

> Within a year or so Jerome was able to present Damasus with the first-fruits of his work—a revision of the text of the four Gospels, where the variations had been extreme. In a covering letter he explained the principles which he followed: he used a relatively good Latin text as the basis for his revision, and compared it with some old Greek manuscripts. He emphasized that he treated the current Latin text [of his day] as conservatively as possible, and changed it only where the meaning was distorted. Though we do not have the Latin manuscripts which Jerome chose as the basis of his work, it appears that they belonged to the European form of the Old Latin (perhaps they were similar to manuscript b). The Greek manuscripts apparently belonged to the Alexandrian type of text. (Metzger 1964, 1968, 1992, 76)

Initially the Jerome Latin translation was well received. However, the critics came out of the woodwork to complain about the supposed liberties that he took in making his translation.

> After I had written my former letter, containing a few remarks on some Hebrew words, a report suddenly reached me that certain contemptible creatures were deliberately assailing me with the charge that I had endeavored to correct passages in the gospels, against the authority of the ancients and the opinion of the whole world.[212]

These condemnations only grew in intensity after the death of Pope Damasus in 384 C.E. The new pope and Jerome did not have a working relationship like he had shared with Damasus, so he made the decision to leave Rome. One again, Jerome was wandering toward the east.

Jerome Becomes a Hebrew Scholar

In 386 C.E. Jerome had found his way to Bethlehem, where he would spend the rest of his life. He was traveling with a few of those who had remained loyal to him, as well as Paula, a well-off woman of nobility from Rome. Paula had grown attracted to the plain and simple way of life without luxury, as a result of Jerome's influence. However, here financial wealth was used to establish a monastery under the direction of Jerome. It would be here that he would take his scholarly pursuits to a whole new level, completing the ultimate work of his life.

---

[212] Jerome, "The Letters of St. Jerome", Volume VI: St. Jerome: Letters and Select Works, ed. Philip Schaff and Henry Wace (New York: Christian Literature Company, 1893), 43-44.

As you likely remember, Jerome's understanding of Hebrew was only functional, so this new life in Bethlehem was going to offer him the opportunity at become an extraordinary Hebrew scholar. Here again, Paula was able to help him afford several different Jewish tutors, who helped him fully grasp a number of the more difficult characteristics of the language. Concerning one teacher, Jerome said;

> What trouble and expense it cost me to get Baraninas to teach me under cover of night. For by his fear of the Jews he presented to me in his own person a second edition of Nicodemus.[213]

The Jews of Jerome's day were not too receptive to Gentiles for their failure to pronounce the guttural sounds properly. This did not dissuade Jerome though, as he simply put more effort into his studies, and was eventually able to master these sounds. In addition, Jerome transliterated numerous Hebrew words into Latin.[214] This method not only assisted him in remembering the words but also preserved the Hebrew pronunciation of that time.

The Greatest Controversy of Jerome

We are not sure how much of the Bible that Damasus wanted Jerome to translate. However, we are well aware of how much Jerome intended to accomplish. Jerome was very attentive and resolute. Jerome was

---

[213] John 3:2; Ibid, Volume VI, 176.

[214] Transliterated means to represent letters or words written in one alphabet using the corresponding letters of another.

determined to make available a revised Latin translation of the whole Bible.

> Therefore, I beseech you, Paula and Eustochium, to pour out your supplications for me to the Lord, that so long as I am in this poor body, I may write something pleasing to you, useful to the Church, worthy of posterity. As for my contemporaries, I am indifferent to their opinions, for they pass from side to side as they are moved by love or hatred.[215]

The basis for the Old Testament was the Greek Septuagint (LXX).[216] The Septuagint was viewed by the Christians of the time as though it too were inspired by God.[217] It functioned as Scripture for the Greek-speaking Jews and was used by a large amount of Christians down to the time of Jesus and his apostles, as well up unto the time of Jerome. In the Greek New Testament, most of the 320 direct quotations and the collective total of

---

[215] Jerome, "Prefaces to the Books of the Vulgate Version of the Old Testament", Second Series, Volume VI: St. Jerome: Letters and Select Works, ed. Philip Schaff and Henry Wace (New York: Christian Literature Company, 1893), 493.

[216] A Greek translation of the Hebrew Bible made 280 and 150 B.C.E. to meet the needs of Greek-speaking Jews outside Palestine. The Septuagint contains some books not in the Hebrew canon. The roman numerals LXX stand for seventy, and according to tradition, The Septuagint was made by 72 Jewish scholars of Alexandria, Egypt. Later, the number 70 somehow came to be used, and thus the version was called the Septuagint.

[217] We need to offer a word of caution here, because the Greek Septuagint was not inspired. Moreover, there were a number of Greek translations made, which was not a carefully guard text, nor unified. Thus, there are considerable differences between the Greek and the Hebrew Old Testament.

perhaps 890 quotations and references to the Hebrew Old Testament are from the Septuagint.

As Jerome got involved in the work of translating the Old Testament, he was again met with discrepancies, like had been the case with the different Latin manuscripts, and now between the different Greek manuscripts he was using. One can only imagine the feeling of disappointment, exasperation, or weariness of this man as he realized the work that would be involved in translating, as well as making textual decisions too. In the end, Jerome simply decided that it would be more practical to scrap his plan of using the Greek manuscripts, and even the revered Septuagint, and to go with the Hebrew text as his basis for the translation.

Here is where Jerome finds himself being falsely accused as a forger of the text, a man who was disrespectful of God, deserting the traditions of the church in favor of the Jews. Even the leading theologian of Jerome's day, Augustine, begged him to drop the Hebrew text and return to the use of the Septuagint as the basis for his Latin translation, saying: "If your translation begins to be more generally read in many churches, it will be a grievous thing that, in the reading of Scripture, differences must arise between the Latin Churches and the Greek Churches."[218]

As you can see the fear that dwelled within Augustine, was the church to become even further divided? He feared that the Western churches would be

---

[218] Augustine of Hippo, "Letters of St. Augustin", trans. J. G. Cunningham In , in A Select Library of the Nicene and Post-Nicene Fathers of the Christian Church, First Series, Volume I: The Confessions and Letters of St. Augustin With a Sketch of His Life and Work, ed. Philip Schaff (Buffalo, NY: Christian Literature Company, 1886), 327.

using Jerome's Latin text based on the Hebrew text, while the Eastern Greek churches would be using the Greek Septuagint. Moreover, Augustine was concerned about setting aside the Greek Septuagint, for a translation that only Jerome would be able to defend.

What was Jerome's reaction to all of these critics? He chose to stay true to himself, he simply ignored them. He stayed with the Hebrew text as the basis for his Latin translation of the Old Testament, and brought the whole Latin Bible to complete in 405 C.E. It would be labeled the Vulgate some years later, which is a reference to a commonly received version (the Latin vulgatus meaning "common, that which is popular").

The Accomplishment of Jerome

The Old Testament portion of the Latin translation that Jerome produced was not just a revision of the current Latin texts. It was the beginning of something far greater, a course change in the way the Bible was studied and translated. "The Vulgate," said historian Will Durant, "remains as the greatest and most influential literary accomplishment of the fourth century." (Durant 1950, 54)

Granted Jerome possessed a bitter or critical manner of speaking and a combative temperament, he by himself transmitted Bible research back to the inspired Hebrew text. With a sharp eye, he pored over and compared ancient Hebrew and Greek manuscripts of the Bible that are no longer accessible to us today. Jerome's monumental work was also accomplished before that of the Jewish Masoretes.[219] Therefore, the Vulgate is a

---

[219] The Masoretes were early Jewish scholars: any of the scholars who produced the Masoretic Text. The Masoretic Text was the Hebrew

treasured reference tool for comparing alternate renderings of Bible texts. Hence, it would seem that his and his fellow assistant's petitions were heard:

> Therefore, I beseech you, Paula and Eustochium, to pour out your supplications for me to the Lord, that so long as I am in this poor body, I may write something pleasing to you, useful to the Church, **worthy of posterity**. As for my contemporaries, I am indifferent to their opinions, for they pass from side to side as they are moved by love or hatred.[220]

Bible: revised and annotated by Jewish scholars between the 6th and 10th centuries C.E.

[220] Jerome, "Prefaces to the Books of the Vulgate Version of the Old Testament", trans. W. H. Fremantle, G. Lewis and W. G. Martley In , in A Select Library of the Nicene and Post-Nicene Fathers of the Christian Church, Second Series, Volume VI: St. Jerome: Letters and Select Works, ed. Philip Schaff and Henry Wace (New York: Christian Literature Company, 1893), 493.

Books Authored by Edward D. Andrews

APPLYING GOD'S WORD MORE FULLY IN YOUR LIFE: How to Broaden and Deepen Your Understanding of God's Word[221]

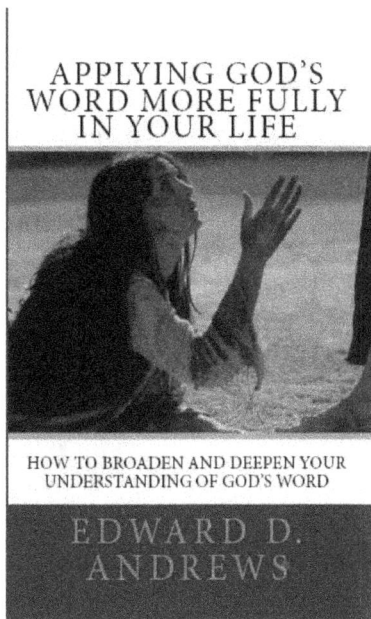

APPLYING GOD'S WORD MORE FULLY IN YOUR LIFE

HOW TO BROADEN AND DEEPEN YOUR UNDERSTANDING OF GOD'S WORD

EDWARD D. ANDREWS

Hundreds of millions of Christians around the world are lacking the basic knowledge of the Bible's teachings. Moreover, they are therefore, unable to take advantage of the full happiness of partaking in joint worship of God; they need to have their powers of discernment trained by constant practice to distinguish good from evil, they need to leave the elementary doctrine of Christ and move on to maturity. This book has been penned for that very purpose, to help all Christians to increase and expand their understanding of God's Word and to apply it more fully in their lives. Be aware that this book will ask questions that are designed, to help us investigate our inner-self.

---

[221] https://www.createspace.com/3829757

MISREPRESENTING JESUS: Debunking Bart D. Ehrman's Misquoting Jesus[222]

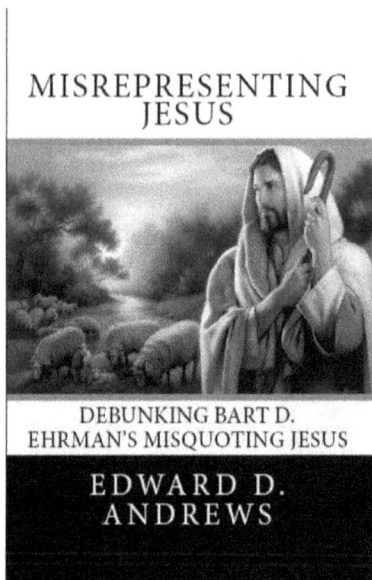

MISREPRESENTING JESUS

DEBUNKING BART D. EHRMAN'S MISQUOTING JESUS

EDWARD D. ANDREWS

Edward Andrews boldly answers the challenges Bart D. Ehrman puts against the divine inspiration and authority of the Bible. By glimpsing into the life of Bart D. Ehrman and following along his course of academic studies, Andrews helps the reader to understand the biases, assumptions, and shortcomings supporting Ehrman's arguments. Using sound logic, technical exegesis, and conservative interpretation, Andrews helps scholars overcome the teachings of biblical errancy that Ehrman propagates.

"A sometimes complex area has been made very palatable and enjoyable to read. Dare I say--even quite exciting!" —Online reviewer

---

222 https://www.createspace.com/3759006

THE TEXT OF THE NEW TESTAMENT: A Beginner's Guide to New Testament Textual Criticism[223]

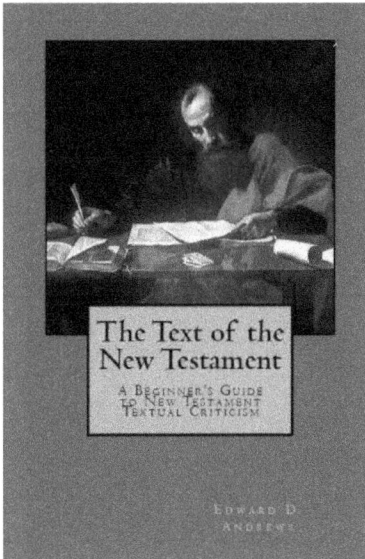

Many critics of the Bible say that we cannot know what was said, because we do not have the originals. This is a false claim, because we can get back to the originals by restoring what was there through the science of textual criticism, and a restored text, is the same as the originals, minus being on the same original papyrus.

Starting with the basics, Edward D. Andrews guides you through New Testament textual criticism. Starting with the threat to the authority and authenticity of the New Testament text (Bible critics), The Text of the New Testament leads you through each aspect of textual studies to prepare you for studying the Bible as a student of the textual history. Even more importantly, Andrews presents arguments to defend the Bible's authority and accuracy against the latest onslaught of atheist and agnostic scholarship undermining the Bible as divinely inspired, inerrant and irrefutable. Andrews gives the student the history of the text, explaining the art and science of textual criticism, offering the reader a word picture of the ancient books,

---

[223] https://www.createspace.com/3789167

as well as the basics of paleography (dating manuscripts). In addition, he explains how we can restore what the original text said, the different methods of textual criticism, taking the reader through the process of publishing the original New Testament books, along with the 1,400-year period of corruption by copyists, culminating with the 400 years of restoration, and so much more. This will enable the Bible student to defend himself against those who wish to cast doubt on the trustworthiness of our Greek New Testament text.

THE COMPLETE GUIDE TO BIBLE TRANSLATION:
Bible Translation Choices and Translation Principles[224]

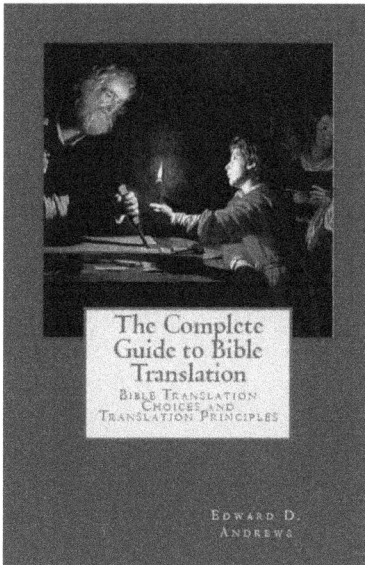

The Complete Guide to Bible Translation

BIBLE TRANSLATION CHOICES AND TRANSLATION PRINCIPLES

EDWARD D. ANDREWS

It is a daunting task for the new Bible student to walk into a store for the purpose of purchasing a Bible. Immediately, he is met with shelves upon shelves of more than 100 different English translation choices: AMP, AT, ASV, BLE, CEB, CEV, ERV, ESV, HCSB, IB, ISV, JB, KJ21, LB, MLB, NAB, NASB, NCV, NEB, NET, NJB, NIV, NIVI, NIRV, NKJV, NLT, NLV, NRSV, REB, RSV, RVB, SEB, TEV, TNIV, WE and on and on. He is even further bewildered when he realizes that, in addition to the standard format, there are different formats within each translation: a reference Bible, a study Bible, a life application Bible, an archaeology Bible. He further notices that some translations claim to be Essentially Literal, while others claim to be Dynamic Equivalent (thought for thought), which only serves to increase his confusion.

The goal of THE COMPLETE GUIDE TO BIBLE TRANSLATION is to offer those new to the subject an

---

[224] https://www.createspace.com/3771321

overview of the history and methods, aims and results of the Bible translation process.

In addition, the reader will gain an appreciation of the work and lifetime efforts of hundreds of Bible scholars over the past 450-years, who have labored, so that we can say that we have many very good translations that are a mirror like reflection of the original, in translation. The reader will also find that he or she has a renewed confidence in the reliability of the Bible. Finally, the reader will be able to determine for himself or herself, which translations are the best for study and research.

YOUR GUIDE FOR DEFENDING THE BIBLE: Self-Education of the Bible Made Easy[225]

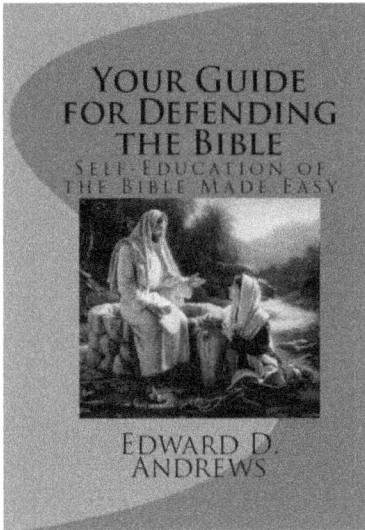

LET ME ASK YOU SOME QUESTIONS:

(1) Do you want to waste your hard-earned money by buying the wrong books?

(2) Do have some basic Bible knowledge, and would love to have more?

(3) Do you wish that you could be better at sharing your faith, defending what you know to be true?

(4) Do you fear those tough Bible questions?

(5) Do you want to be able to defend God's Word as true, inerrant and inspired?

(6) Are you tired of the Bible scholars having all the knowledge?

(7) Do you want to have confidence when you are talking to others about the Bible?

(8) Do you want to learn how to study better, and more efficiently?

---

[225] https://www.createspace.com/3764440

(9) Do you want to accomplish these things in the most productive way possible?

If one were to go on any discussion board on the worldwide internet, he or she would find hundreds of millions in ongoing, unending debates on countless websites about God's Word and its reliability and inspiration. In other words, 'is the Bible the Word of God?' Sadly, the reader of this book will find many people today, who are losing faith in the belief that the Bible is the inspired, inerrant Word of God. Why?

Liberal-progressive Christianity has overtaken conservative Christianity in the last 70-years. These are the ones, who claim that the Bible is a book by man alone, not inspired; being subject to errors, contradictions, and "unscientific." Other critics argue that the Bible is nothing more than a collection of myths and legends. Still, others argue that archaeology and Biblical chronology cannot be harmonized. Other critics claim that the Gospels of Mathew, Mark, Luke and John are not historically accurate. Others still, argue that Jesus was not divine, claiming he was merely a traveling sage.

Your Guide for Defending the Bible offers the Bible student an introduction to many different subject areas that will help him or her to follow the following biblical counsel:

BE PREPARED TO MAKE A DEFENSE

1 Peter 3:15 English Standard Version (ESV)

But in your hearts honor Christ the Lord as holy, always being prepared to make a defense to anyone who asks you for a reason for the hope that is in you

CONTEND FOR THE FAITH

Jude 1:3 English Standard Version (ESV)

Beloved, although I was very eager to write to you about our common salvation, I found it necessary to write appealing to you to contend for the faith that was once for all delivered to the saints.

HELP THOSE WHO DOUBT

Jude 1:22-23 English Standard Version (ESV)

And have mercy on those who doubt; save others by snatching them out of the fire;

AN INTRODUCTION TO BIBLE DIFFICULTIES: So-called Errors and Contradictions[226]

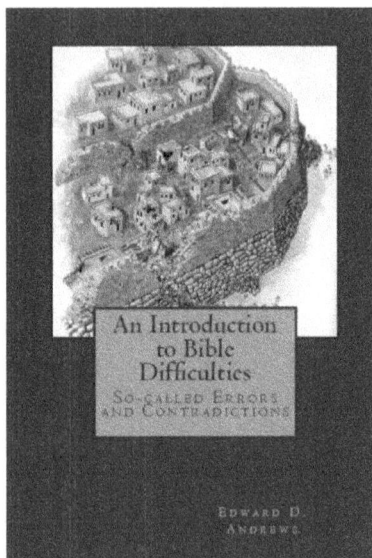

The Bible is loaded with thousands of difficult, challenging passages-many of which become obstacles in the development of our faith. These difficulties arise out of differences in culture, language, needs, religious and political organization, not to mention between 2,000 and 3,500 years of separation. Calling attention to these difficulties and sifting out the misconceptions, Edward Andrews defends the inerrancy of the Bible, clarifies apparent contradictions, and arms you with what you need to defend your faith in the Bible.

---

[226] https://www.createspace.com/3796775